FLAVOUR

A world of beautiful food

FARM
annual

FLAVOUR

A world of beautiful food

Vicky Bhogal

H

HODDER &
STOUGHTON

First published in Great Britain in 2009 by Hodder & Stoughton

An Hachette UK company

A CIP catalogue record for this title is available from the British Library

ISBN 978 0 340 96318 0

Design by Lisa Pettibone
Typeset in Din Mittleshrift and Univers45
Illustrations © Karin Akesson
Photographs © Gus Filgate
Additional photographic sources:
Alamy Images: Walter Bibikow ii, 113 & 183, BroadSpektrum 77, Jim Cole 65 (left), Chad Ehlers 64, Rebecca Erol 136, 147, Mark Higgins 182, Russell Kord 137 (top), Martin Lee 30, PCL 23 (middle) & 219, Alex Ramsay 23 (top), Isabelle Rozenbaum 179 (right), Sue Wilson 179 (left).
Rex Features: Patrick Rideaux 65 (right).

Printed and bound by Mohn Media in Germany

Hodder & Stoughton policy is to use papers that are natural, renewable and recyclable products and made from wood grown in sustainable forests. The logging and manufacturing processes are expected to conform to the environmental regulations of the country of origin.

Hodder & Stoughton Ltd
338 Euston Road
London NW1 3BH
www.hodder.co.uk

DEDICATION

To all my sisters who taste everything with me,
from bitter to sweet, and never complain of feeling full.

And to my fearless Father who also, by naming
me Vicky, seems to have set the wheel of fusion in
motion right from the very beginning...

CONTENTS

INTRODUCTION

'WELL, THE WAY I SEE IT, whether you write it or not, whether you use that word or not, the fact is, it's how you cook. I mean, it's just how you are anyway, isn't it? That's what I think.'

Earnestly, and kindly, Kate leaned across her half-eaten cupcake towards me to emphasise her point, a massacre of crumbs tumbling to the plate from her cream-cheese-frosted fingertips.

'Actually, you know what? I think your shopping just about sums it up.' She laughed as she craned her head round the counter. 'It's all there, in a couple of bags. Don't you think?'

At the foot of my stool lay a filmy blue-and-white-striped carrier bag, and a much larger, stuffed-to-the-brim shopper with fraying jute handles and a large ink stain splaying out of one corner where a pen reached the end of its days. The bags contained the fruits of our shopping trip this morning along the Portobello Road. Several tall, majestic bunches of holy basil, a slim packet of razor-thin beef carpaccio from the butcher, a few pink dragonfruit,

glossy plum tomatoes, some globe artichokes, perfumed Indian mangoes, a treasure trove of nine spice packets including rust-coloured sumac and wrinkly sunburnt chillies, organic potatoes, a loaf of ciabatta, sherbet lemons and a bottle of olive oil.

Maybe she had a point. We were perched on stools in a bakery, a tiny slice of cupcake heaven in west London, restoring our blood-sugar levels after much trudging. It was summer 2007. The 'it' she was referring to being written was this book, a fledgling idea I was exploring and discussing with her. The 'word' was 'fusion', often seen as the real 'f-word' in the world of cookery, wildly misunderstood and misinterpreted, much to my frustration, and thus the subject of our conversation.

I LOVE COOKING. But first and foremost I love eating. Yes, the enjoyment of eating is the thing. The cooking is a close second, and necessary to bring to fruition whatever I desire to eat. And it has been the same ever since I was little. Food and cooking were such a part of my upbringing that it is impossible to disentangle them from my childhood memories. This is why I wrote my first cookery book, *Cooking Like Mummyji*, a love letter to the wonderful Indian food I was grateful to be fed and taught how to cook by my family over the years. It seemed wrong somehow not to try to preserve their delicious recipes and share them with others, just as they had lovingly shared them over the years with me, their wide-eyed, humble apprentice.

Indian home cooking is my culinary soul. It is joy, comfort, nostalgia, roots and medicine to me. However, it is food in general, in all its diversity, that bewitched me right from the beginning and still holds me enthralled to this day.

I was lucky to enjoy mouth-watering and wholesome traditional Punjabi cuisine at home, but my family were also keen on eating and cooking all sorts of dishes, embracing new flavours and techniques as they came across them. My mother would effortlessly intertwine all sorts of meals over the course of a week, ensuring not just a nutritional balance but also one of flavours and textures. Pies and casseroles were as much part of my intake as steaming hot, papery rotia, straight from the flames into my thali. The food that we came across in school, through friends, in the supermarkets and then later in restaurants and on holidays was absorbed into our daily diet and became who we were. Layer by delicate layer, a millefeuille of culinary identity was created.

This had always seemed completely normal to me until I began to be asked if I ever ate, or cooked, food other than Indian. This seemed such a strange question. I think, if you love food, you love food, all types, and I don't conduct a sort of culinary passport control, checking the origins of a dish or ingredient or flavour before I can stamp it as approved to sit on my plate. I welcome new visitors with open arms and as much hospitality and warmth as the dear, trusted old friends of my store cupboards.

And I am delighted by the fact that in the little corner of the metropolis I have made my own, I am able to draw from a rich, sprawling heritage of centuries of ingredients traversing their way across the globe. That with a flick of a lid or stir of a spoon, I can add the perfumed whisper of a Persian court, an echo of cool pine forests at twilight or the faint tap of a tango on cobbled alleyways to my daily urban life, while the cars roar by outside in the dark depths of the evening.

I feel lucky and am grateful to have access to such a wide variety of ingredients, more of which are being stocked in mainstream stores than ever before. By this, I am not referring necessarily to fresh produce, the complex arguments about which could easily fill a book of their own (for, as with much in life, things are rarely as black and white as they seem on first sight). For should we not be supporting local and seasonal produce? Very much so. But what would that mean in the depths of our winters when we cannot bear the sight of any more potatoes and cabbages? And can we afford to be, and indeed is it right to be, so nationalistic when our lives have become so globally inter-dependent? How do we choose between one farmer's right to a livelihood over another's, especially those disadvantaged by lopsided trade rules? And is it better to put on our plates that which has travelled many times up and down our country by road, with a carbon footprint weightier than that arriving by sea? Or is it about freshness, in which case maybe we should be self-sufficient and eat only what we grow ourselves.

Oh, but then the winter's yield of cabbages serves to deprive and depress me again. As with most things, balance, common sense and fairness, rather than extremism, go a long way.

When I talk about the wealth of ingredients we have at our fingertips these days, I am not so much referring to fresh produce or specialist delis as to the myriad of dry goods, spices, sauces and flavourings available even in the most ordinary supermarket, in the quaintest town. And if you were to walk into any kitchen in Britain and fling open the cabinet doors, chances are you would find lithe bottles of moss-green olive oil nestling alongside dusky soy sauce; sweetly pungent vanilla extract next to incendiary pots of chilli powder; musky dried oregano next to lip-smarting malt vinegar. Here they stand in close proximity, a multicultural assortment, like commuters on the Tube. And just like commuters, never making eye contact, getting off at their relative stops without a glance or a smile.

Too often, the ingredients we have in our cupboards are not explored in day-to-day cooking even as single flavourings, let alone used together outside traditional pairings. Some flavourings, often the ones that were bought distant months ago because a specific recipe needed half a teaspoon, we no longer know what to do with. They silently sit in the gloom, waiting perhaps to be used for that dish once again, but more often than not enduring a slow, dusty demise in the ingredient graveyard.

I am quite dismayed by this, as it seems such a shame not only for it to go to waste, but also for us not to fully enjoy what we have in our cupboards or on our supermarket shelves. Such a shame not to be completely aware of the transformative and versatile properties of the bottles and tubs on the shelves before us, which can enliven our meals and our taste buds so alchemically.

And so, as I continued to cook away in my normal daily life, feeding family, friends and, most importantly and most often, myself, using a cooking style fuelled mostly by greed but also insatiable curiosity, it was pointed out to me that perhaps these recipes could form the basis of a new book. A book that would celebrate, use and combine ingredients from around the world in new ways and get the most out of them.

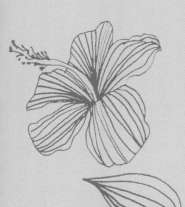

IN COOKING as in other areas of life, we have our own style and repertoire. A confident, adventurous cook might be at ease with bold flavours. Another might prefer subtle, delicate flavours. It's a matter of taste, and this, even in the most literal sense, is not that easy to define. We've all heard of tastes being divided into salt, sweet, bitter, sour. Many people now add a fifth: umami, which refers to a satisfying savoury meatiness or protein-like quality, most often found in fermented foods but also in aged cheeses and even vegetables such as tomatoes. Culture makes its mark, too. In China, a fifth taste of 'spicy' is added to the basic four. Indians hold there to be six basic tastes: sweet, sour, salt, bitter, hot/pungent and astringent, and, according to the ancient Ayurvedic health system, for optimum digestion all six should be represented at each meal. In ancient times, Aristotle referred to two essential tastes – sweet and bitter, with the sub-tastes of pungent, salty, succulent, harsh, sour and the beautifully self-explanatory puckery.

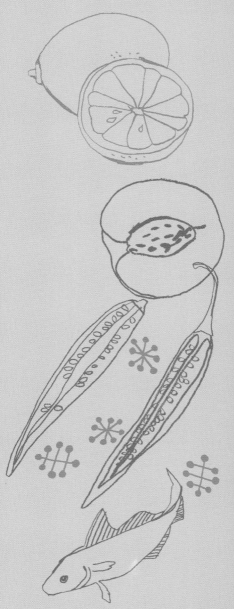

SALT: feta, halloumi, anchovies, preserved olives, capers, soy sauce, miso, bacon

SWEET: fruit, sugars, honey, wine, cream, milk, butter, high-starch vegetables such as potatoes, carrots, sweetcorn and parsnips; some fish and seafood, such as monkfish and lobster; some nuts, such as chestnuts

BITTER: unsweetened coffee, unsweetened chocolate, certain gourd vegetables, paan betel nut, citrus peel, garam masala, paprika, kale, chicory, radish

SOUR: tamarind, lemon, lime, sumac, live yoghurt, vinegar

UMAMI: miso, soy sauce, tofu, Worcestershire sauce, tomatoes, meat, mushrooms, anchovy sauce, Parmesan, roquefort, potatoes, bacon, ketchup, Marmite and Vegemite, meat and fish stocks

Beyond these, the senses and the imagination can take us further: to pungent and peppery, such as ginger and some olive oils; to agrodolce (sweet and sour), such as tamarind, balsamic vinegar and pomegranate; to salty sour, such as gherkins and pickled chillies; salt umami, such as fish sauce, bacon and anchovy sauce; sweet umami, such as tomatoes and potatoes; sweet astringent, such as cranberries; citric, tart and tangy, such as lemon, lemongrass, lime, lemon thyme and bergamot; woody and earthy, such as anise, cloves, nutmeg, mushrooms, rosemary; creamy, anything from cheese to chestnuts, bananas and coconut; warm and aromatic, such as cinnamon, allspice; even such a category as fresh, clean and light, which might encompass cucumber, mint leaf and starfruit.

Salt itself is like an alarm clock for the taste buds, preparing them for receiving and registering the flavours of food. Everyone's taste buds are different, and different people require different levels of salt. I've learnt through experience always to advise people to use the amounts of salt appropriate to them, which requires, as ever, tasting and checking.

Ingredients can share characteristics, or flavour profiles, no matter where they originate from or where they are now commonly used. Thus, although lemongrass and lemon might be botanically quite different, and belong to different national cuisines and dishes, they both have a citric profile and thus can be used in similar ways, one substituting for another to achieve a subtle change. Some ingredients need other tastes to unlock and release their flavour. If you try garam masala on its own on the tongue, it tastes dusty. Add a touch of salt and it is transformed to aromatic. Paprika tastes bitter alone but then completely different with a drop of the acidity of lemon juice.

Flavours can also change not just according to what you pair them with but also through cooking techniques. Raw cumin seeds taste unpleasant, but dry-roast them for a few seconds in a hot pan or sizzle them in oil and their true flavour emerges. Bite into raw onion and it tastes eye-wateringly sharp and peppery. When slowly cooked and browned, the fibres break down, the natural sugars are released and caramelised, and the taste is rounded and sweetened. Aubergines can be bitter raw but when roasted in their skins, the flavour can change to a smoky umami taste. Freezing, on the other hand, can dull the sweetness of a dish while intensifying acidity. An ice cream or sorbet needs to be sweeter before freezing than you would like the finished product to taste.

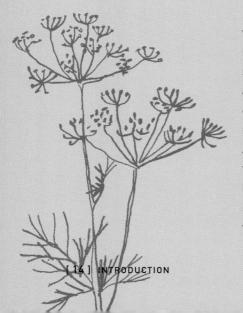

Some tastes and flavour profiles complement others. A touch of balsamic will bring out the sweetness of ripe strawberries. I might highlight the herby quality of basil by combining it with creamy pine nuts in a pesto, to serve with neutral gnocchi, say, or I might combine it with lemon to bring out its citrus notes. Creaminess – not water or sugar – works well in reducing heat. Gulping water down when you've eaten too much chilli doesn't help at all, and might even make it worse, but yoghurt or coconut milk will work to reduce heat: whether added in the cooking or consumed alongside. Not for nothing are yoghurt drinks, and especially salty ones, a feature of the national cuisines of some very hot countries.

I haven't talked much about 'hot' for chillies. Technically, this isn't a flavour but a physical sensation. Capsaicin, which is contained in chillies, causes a sensation of burning in the mouth, and this reaction combines with our taste reception. This in turn triggers the release of endorphins, compensating for the 'pain' in a similar way to the effect of morphine, leading to the pleasure that the brain registers upon eating chilli, and which is thought to be why chillies can, for some people, be addictive. This is also believed to be why the threshold for chilli can increase over time.

Balance and proportion are important. My favourite approach is to work with three flavours: maybe in a classic combination that is subtly adjusted by using alternatives with similar profiles, such as apple and mint with lemongrass instead of lemon, or by taking a classic pair and adding an unexpected third (perhaps one that has a known relationship to one of the existing pair), such as lime, basil and mandarin, or tomato, balsamic and cumin. The third ingredient is often, although not always, used in less intensity than the main two. I don't usually use more than three main flavours. There might be other flavours in a dish, but they will be there in supporting roles.

For many of the recipes in this book I have described the process that went into their creation: what inspired them, what kind of result I was after and why I combined the flavours that I did. All the dishes come from the starting point of the flavours themselves and not the national background of ingredients. I also suggest, at the end of most of the recipes, how you can substitute other ingredients with a similar flavour profile or take the dish in a different direction.

I have given weight, volume and size measurements for the recipes, but don't rely solely on the numbers, judge with your eyes too. Train yourself to assess quantities visually. This, along with developing and trusting your palate, will eventually free you to cook more spontaneously, just as previous generations were able. Then, when you create new recipes for yourself, as I hope you will do, use all of your senses. Cooking is not just about what happens in your mouth. Look at the colours you are putting together, the physical textures of the ingredients, be guided by the sound they make to let you know, for example, if they are crisp enough, and, as with tasting wine, smell your ingredients and finished dishes to fully appreciate them and to learn to recognise the flavours in their glorious entirety. I mostly cook with simple techniques, so that nothing detracts from the flavours, which for me are the most important thing. When you are trying out new flavours for yourself, use them in a technique you are already confident of.

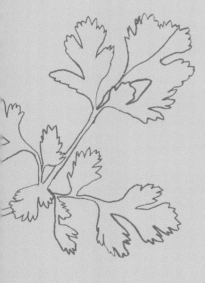

NONE OF THE RECIPES in Flavour was created for the sake of it. They were all born out of genuine hunger and curiosity on my part. Although some of the ingredients will be a little harder to come across than others, the majority can be found in any large supermarket; the rest, included for those who want to be a little more adventurous, can be found online or at an ethnic supermarket. A lot of these ingredients, especially spices, keep well in the cupboard or can be frozen, and so it is both worthwhile and enjoyable to make a trip to a Japanese or Indian or Thai supermarket and stock up once in a while – now that you have in your hands some inspiration for how to use them outside of the obvious dishes, and won't bin them after a solitary teaspoonful.

Cooking with unfamiliar ingredients or combining familiar ingredients in unfamiliar ways can feel like food Russian roulette, which is risky when you are hungry. However, with a focus on simplicity and only a couple of flavours at a time, the rewards can be great. Building confidence and trusting your palate is wonderfully freeing, taking enjoyment of food to another level and igniting infinite new food possibilities, rather than eating what someone else deems you should like. I've never much gone for blind faith or absolutism in anything. Of course, everyone needs guidance and a framework when they start to learn something new, but where this can take you is limitless and up to you, and, crucially, *for* you.

And this is what Kate reminded me of over our cake break that day, which made me finally decide to put this book together.

The simple fact is that although it is right and respectful to uphold culinary traditions, food has been fused since the beginnings of civilisation. Over millennia, ingredients have travelled out of their homelands and across the globe with everyone from pioneers to pirates, scoring their trajectories across maps amid war, colonisation, mission, trade, survival, adventure, slavery, conquest and exploration. Of course, all ingredients were originally indigenous to a particular part of the world, yet it is near impossible to find a national cuisine constructed solely from ingredients born and bred in the homeland.

What I find interesting is the way in which new ingredients and flavours were embraced but techniques and style often remained traditional. This, to me, is elegant and honest fusion. Being open and welcoming, learning about the new and innovative, yet also upholding tradition and not compromising identity. The two elements complementing and enriching each other, without competing or diluting.

If Indians had sat in their corner, at arm's length from the odd-looking curved chillies the Portuguese had brought, which Columbus called 'the pepper of the Indies', eyeing them up suspiciously and saying: 'Er, no, sorry, wouldn't be authentic to use those, I'll stick with the black pepper, thanks,' then almost all of the Indian dishes familiar to us in Britain today simply wouldn't exist. Someone had to make the first bold move and put the chilli with the turmeric. We all know the rest.

Borders have been drawn and redrawn throughout history. Perhaps with cooking there are now no borders at all: we can enjoy the tastes of many parts of the world in our own homes very easily, whenever we like.

I am not a chef of any description. I am a home cook, taught by family initially and then self-taught, who has committed her recipes to paper and print. That's all. I hugely admire chefs, but I am not one, nor do I have any desire to be one. I learn what I need to at my own pace and as the recipe requires, and so can you.

Home-cooking is not competitive cooking, unless you have serious issues. It is about the food you, your friends and family enjoy. Every so often I try something new, sometimes out of curiosity, sometimes out of the necessity to use something up, but I only cook it for myself, freezing leftovers if needed. I tend not to try new dishes out on other people straight away. Cooking for guests can be stressful and can reduce anyone to a bag of nerves, so save your most confident cooking for then. Once I'm happy with a new dish, then I introduce it to friends. Whatever didn't work has also added to my store of knowledge. It will be the same for you. Ultimately, your taste and your opinion are what matters.

The one thing I am sure of is that you, just because you're reading this, have a genuine love of food and a passion for cookery, which is not dependent upon what style it is or what your background is, or whether you have a deli or farmer's market nearby or live in the country rearing your own meat, or how much technique you know or whether you frequent fancy restaurants. A person who loves cooking can always create gastronomic magic.

My love as ever,

COOK'S NOTES

THERE IS A SPANISH SAYING, *Cada cabeza es un mundo,* which loosely means that every person's mind is a whole world unto itself. This phrase neatly expresses my cooking philosophy, in that through following your taste buds and with a little imagination and practice, the unique flavours of your cooking can be celebrated, enjoyed and shared with others, bringing a bit of you to every plate you serve.

I hope that Flavour will give you the confidence to experiment with your cooking. If this feels daunting, don't worry. Start simply by using the flavour combinations you have enjoyed in one dish in a slightly different method that you are comfortable with. For example, if you like Jaffa Cakes, why not try baking cookies made with a few spoonfuls of marmalade stirred into the mixture and studded with some chocolate chips? Or mini trifles of broken sponge fingers in an orange jelly topped with a rich chocolate custard and finished with a little fresh cream? Then try changing one ingredient to see if you like it, such as using white chocolate instead. Or keep the same method and textures but change the flavours instead.

Measurements are the key to all this. Getting them wrong can mean a potentially great flavour combination falls apart. Measuring scales are necessary, especially in baking, but practice, and constantly tasting, is crucial too. I often measure my ingredients by eye. But it takes a while to learn how to do this. You can make a start by taking notice of how much volume the number on the scales equates to. Once you've got an idea of what quantities look like, try measuring ingredients in spoons or cup measures. It will make the whole process feel quicker – and it gives you the freedom to start substituting ingredients of the same volume and consistency.

With practice comes a sense of rhythm and familiarity. Gradually you will get a feel for exactly how to use your utensils and equipment – how much pressure to employ, how long it takes for your oven to heat up, exactly how to hold your knife for the best grip. All these subtle little differences will have an impact on how the recipe turns out.

When you cook recipes, sometimes the results might vary slightly. Think about why this could be and adapt a little. For example, when I made my passionfruit and white chocolate cookies recently at a friend's home, the fruit was slightly smaller than usual, so keeping an eye on how much passionfruit there should be in the mixture I added a couple more. If the fruit is more tart than usual, add a bit more sugar.

Experimenting with items you are planning to throw away gives you even more freedom to try something new, whilst also cutting back on waste. Overripe strawberries destined for the dustbin and a little left-over crème fraiche or yoghurt in the fridge? Why not whiz together and grind in a touch of black pepper then freeze for an unusual frozen yoghurt? Stale bread? Why not tear the few remaining slices into strips, bake until golden on a tray and then whiz into breadcrumbs with some rosemary and a drizzle of extra virgin olive oil, freezing until needed for a savoury crumble topping or to coat some chicken?

Flavour soups with parmesan rinds instead of salt, freeze leftover egg whites in bags for future recipes, such as mousses, and combine the last spoonfuls of jars of seasonings into some softened butter and freeze to use at a later date.

A few last, practical points before you start cooking:

- The eggs I use are medium unless stated otherwise.
- I tend to use salted butter for savoury dishes, and obviously unsalted butter for desserts.
- Get to know your oven; if you use a fan oven the cooking time will be slightly reduced and no pre-heating is needed.
- A lot of spices, especially better value ones from ethnic grocers, come in packets. Try to keep them as fresh as possible by decanting into small screw-top clear jars, marking with little sticky labels that you can soak off at a later date.
- When boiling vegetables, place all root vegetables in cold water and bring to the boil, and all other vegetables that grow above the ground go straight into boiling water. Keep your green vegetables bright by thoroughly salting the cooking water.
- If you don't know how to cut and prepare meat and fish, don't let that stop you from trying a dish. Make the most of butchers and fishmongers, including those in supermarkets, and get them to show you how to do it. Or let them do it for you!

BEFORE

These are the dishes I like to serve as starters, although, of course, they can be eaten alone too at any time you like. Some can be enjoyed as snacks or small meals, others are perfect for sharing with family, friends and a few drinks at gatherings.

The Scallops with Bitter Lemon and Lychee work well passed around on little sticks with some freshly-shaken cocktails, or you could serve a few on a plate as a starter with a little of the sauce drizzled across the seared discs of flesh. I like to serve the Tiger Prawn and Mandarin Soup in petite china cups before some steamed fish or you could ladle the aromatic goodness into an extra large bowl just for yourself to lift your spirits after a bad day. The Chicken Cakes with Seaweed and Lime make cute party nuggets but also try them shaped into larger patties, sandwiched in a freshly-baked bun and served with the crispiest chips and ketchup for a weekend lunch.

TO SHARE
Chorizo Crisps
Peach, Saffron and Tarragon Salsa
Goat's Cheese and Pickled Chilli Dip
Scallops with Bitter Lemon and Lychee
Watermelon Sushi with Balsamic Dipping Water
Cajun Spice Beer Butter Prawns with Sourdough
Arancini with Green Pepper and Green Chilli Butter
Sweet Potato Mini Pasties

IN A BOWL
Ginger Chicken Soup with Lemon and Artichoke
Gin and Herb Broth
Chilled Macadamia and Black Olive Soup
Tiger Prawn and Mandarin Soup
Roasted Carrot Soup with Nectarine and Red Pepper Salsa
Pea and Lemongrass Soup
Sweet Basil Pesto
Pasta with Walnuts and Chilli

SALADS
Buttermilk-soaked Chicken with Ciabatta, Butter Beans
   and Brazils
Grilled Goat's Cheese Salad with Hazelnuts, Pomegranate
   and a Blueberry Dressing
Clove Salt Beef with Figs, Watermelon Pepper Jelly and
   Radicchio

SMALL PLATES
Chickpea Fritters with Beetroot, Buffalo Mozzarella and
   Pink Pepper
Roast Acorn Squash with Pear and Kiwi Chutney
Chicken Cakes with Seaweed and Lime
Paneer Rosemary Spears with Bitter Orange and Almond

Chorizo Crisps

SERVES 4
1 packet chorizo slices

I make these brittle magenta discs when I want the crispy, saltiness of pepperoni on pizza, but without the rest of the pizza. I use the Iberian meat, moist with smoky amber juices, to scoop up small amounts of fresh dips and garlicky-lemony hummus, served alongside swollen kalamata olives. At first I would make these by laying slices on a sheet of foil and browning them under the grill until bubbling and crisp. However, one day, my oven and grill broke down and, in the couple of days it took to fix, I decided to try making these in a hot, dry, non-stick frying pan instead. It was just as easy as the grill option, and quicker, as I didn't have to wait for the grill to heat up. It is now the only way I make them.

Heat a non-stick frying pan and dry-fry the chorizo in batches of a single layer of slices at a time. Cook until bubbling and browned underneath and then lift out (no need to turn and dry-fry the other side), allowing to turn crisp as they cool down.

Try crumbling the cooled, crisped chorizo into scrambled eggs or an omelette, or perhaps on top of soups or into crushed new potatoes with home-made salad cream, or add the salty shards to egg mayonnaise for sandwiches. You may like to try pan-crisping other meats, too, such as Parma ham or salami slices.

Peach, Saffron and Tarragon Salsa

SERVES 2–4
generous pinch of saffron strands
2 tsp mild olive oil
2 ripe peaches, in small chunks
1 tbsp finely chopped fresh
    tarragon
black pepper

Cashmere-soft peaches deserve to be admired and shared. Heavy with juice, they will perfectly partner the chorizo crisps, whipped goat's cheese and pickled chilli dip (page 30), torn toasted pitta and jugfuls of icy fresh lemonade. Perfect for a small, impromptu kitchen lunch with friends.

In sultry weather, I like a hint of exoticism to underlie a more vital herby savoury freshness in my salsa. A touch of saffron is a good choice, given that it is not a woody spice, but has an enveloping musky softness and glorious colour to complement the golden flesh of the peach.

For the leaf, I could have chosen, say, coriander, parsley or chervil, but I decided on tarragon. Referred to as 'the king of herbs' in France, it was introduced to Europe by the Mongol warriors. To them it was known as 'the little dragon', and the name 'tarragon' is thought to have come from the Arabic for little dragon, *tarkhum*. I was told darkly, by a friend who

grows it, that it will strangle itself if not regularly divided. The French, however, gave it the generic name of Artemisia, from the Greek goddess of the moon Artemis, thinking the long tapered leaves looked as though they had been dipped in moonlight.

Tarragon's aniseed flavour gives bite and definition to the sweetness of the fruit, while its grassiness brings a sense of the countryside to the bowl. For me, this dish is like eating a ripe, sticky peach while sitting barefoot in a field at sunset.

Steep the saffron in 1 teaspoon of hot water for about 10 minutes. When cool, stir in the olive oil. Mix the peaches with the tarragon in a bowl, pour in the saffron oil and grind some black pepper over.

Perhaps use a touch of orange-blossom water instead of the saffron, or a little ground coriander. This salsa would also be quite lovely with some grilled chicken wrapped in a warm tortilla, or some grilled lamb chops and new potatoes, or a slab of mature cheddar and crackers.

SINCE THEY ALWAYS SEEMED so quintessentially European to me (Peach Melba being one of my earliest dessert memories, and peaches and cream a firm favourite), I was surprised to learn that peaches are believed to originate in China, where scribes were recording enjoyment of their lusciousness, particularly the white-fleshed varieties, as early as the tenth century BC. They were synonymous with fertility, luck, protection and abundance. Indeed, brides there still carry bunches of the beautiful blossoms to this day.

During the seventeenth century, the peach became popular in England and France. The French, in particular, fell madly in love with the fruit, bestowing on it names of feminine beauty such as Téton de Vénus. Louis XIV was so enamoured by the peach that he awarded a pension to the man who gave him those from Montreuil, a Paris suburb claiming to produce the very best espaliered variety.

Goat's Cheese and Pickled Chilli Dip

SERVES 2–4

250g mild Welsh soft goat's
  cheese

150g Greek yoghurt

2 tsp extra virgin olive oil

2 tsp cumin seeds

½ tsp dried chilli flakes

6 finely chopped green pickled
  chillies from a bottle
  (a.k.a. hot green peppers)

juice of half a lime

3 tbsp chopped fresh coriander

One day, when my sister and I missed the shops after a long day out, I made this dip with what I had in the kitchen. I added woody cumin seeds to some goat's cheese and, thinking of the combination of cream cheese and capers, which I did not have, I added the heat and tanginess of bottled Turkish pickled chillies to cut through the whipped creaminess. I had once eaten something similar in Cairo, called, rather straightforwardly, spicy cheese, with unleavened bread. We gratefully ate ours up with chorizo crisps (page 26) and, between yawns, agreed it was possibly even tastier.

Whip the goat's cheese with the Greek yoghurt in a food processor or with a whisk until smooth.

Heat the oil in a pan with the cumin seeds on a lowish heat, then, when sizzling, add the chilli flakes, stir a couple of times and quickly turn out into the cheese mixture (so as not to let the chilli burn in the pan). Stir well. Add the pickled chillies, lime juice and coriander, stir and serve.

You could add lime zest to the whipped goat's cheese, or finely chopped pepperdew peppers. Or how about oregano and deseeded chopped tomato? Or walnuts, pomegranate and parsley? You can eat the dish as a dip, spread it on bread or bruschetta, or use it to stuff mushrooms, a boned joint of meat, or spread under the skin of a whole spatchcocked chicken. Or mix it with breadcrumbs and use it to stuff whole peppers.

Scallops with Bitter Lemon and Lychee

Hot, sweet, bitter and sour are combined here to complement each other but ultimately to enhance the pure, simple sweetness of the seared scallops, straight out of the pan. The sauce itself should be quite thin so that just the sheerest of layers clings to the expanse of hot skewered flesh after brief dunking. As always, increase or decrease the chilli to your own level of comfort.

Whizz the lychees in a food processor with the bitter lemon until you have a sauce with very finely chopped pieces of lychee. Stir in the basil and both kinds of chilli, then refrigerate while you cook the scallops.

Heat a little oil in a non-stick frying pan. Sear the scallops for 2–3 minutes on each side until golden but still juicy in the middle. Serve at once with cocktail sticks and little bowls of the lychee dipping sauce.

Sometimes I make this with cloudy lemonade instead. You could try a sauce made with fresh strawberries, whizzed with a touch of crushed and dry-roasted Sichuan pepper. Or how about ginger ale, with grated or the thinnest sticks of fresh ginger and chopped fresh coriander? Or tomato with a drop of tamarind or a balsamic glaze.

SERVES 6–10

425g can of lychees, drained (drained weight 200g)
120ml bitter lemon (the mixer drink)
1 tsp finely chopped basil
a couple of pinches of red chilli powder
1 tsp dried red chilli flakes
oil for frying (I use mild olive oil)
scallops for your number of guests (I serve 4 per person)

Watermelon Sushi with Balsamic Dipping Water

SERVES 4–6 (MAKES 28 SLICES)

150g sushi rice

1 tbsp sushi seasoning or rice
wine vinegar

2 sheets of dried seaweed (I use
roasted seaweed)

a couple of wedges of
watermelon

2 tsp rich balsamic glaze (this is
the sweeter, thicker balsamic
that comes in squeezy bottles,
as opposed to the much more
acidic vinegar)

pickled ginger, to serve

Inspired by an article I read about watermelon 'steak' being served in the USA in a similar fashion to seared tuna, I decided to incorporate the fruit into a version of sushi to appeal to my vegetarian guests, who love the vinegared rice, the sushi itself, but not the sashimi fish. Maki sushi, such as this recipe, is sushi rice rolled and wrapped in dried seaweed, which is called nori. Thus, these can also be called nori-maki rolls.

I visit my local Japanese store for supplies, entering into what, in some aisles, feels like a vibrant Manga cartoon. I am guided by staff to the best quality ingredients, nothing lost in translation. Later I roll up the crisp, juicy, ruby watermelon flesh in the savoury saltiness of the sticky rice, served with sweetly tart balsamic water in an abundant platter to be shared by many busy chopsticks. Unfortunately, my friends and I are not polite and serene, our chopsticks bumping into each other as we chatter.

Rinse the rice thoroughly in cold water. Drain and place in a saucepan with 250ml cold water. Bring to the boil, cover and simmer on a very low heat for about 15 minutes or until all the water has been absorbed. Remove from the heat.

Spread the rice evenly on a clean metal tray. Dress with the sushi seasoning, turning with a fork. Leave to cool or fan until the rice is at room temperature.

Place a sheet of seaweed on a bamboo sushi mat with the rough side facing up to help the rice to stick. Have a dipping bowl of water to hand and dip your fingers each time you want to touch or handle the rice. The rice is sticky and will adhere to your fingers unless they are damp. Spread half the rice over three-quarters of the sheet of seaweed, leaving the quarter furthest away from you plain.

Cut pieces of watermelon into sticks about 1cm wide, and as long as possible. Ideally, you would have one long piece the width of the sushi roll, but this is difficult to do without it breaking, so line up the pieces along the rice instead, to make one horizontal layer 1cm thick. Roll the seaweed up tightly and carefully, enclosing the watermelon in the rice, using the mat to help you. Then repeat with the remainder of the rice and watermelon and the second sheet of seaweed. You may have watermelon left over. I just eat it.

Using a wet, sharp knife, cut the rolls into slices just over a centimetre thick. You should get about 14 slices per roll. Wet the knife each time after cutting to ensure a clean, sharp slice. Do not refrigerate before serving, but you can wrap in cling film.

Mix the balsamic glaze in a bowl with 4 tablespoons of water, stirring to combine well. Serve the sushi rolls with the balsamic dipping water and some pickled ginger.

For a sweeter version, you could use other fruits, such as lychee, papaya, mango or pear, and serve with a raspberry dipping sauce with a bit of tamarind, or orange juice with orange-blossom water and mint. For another savoury vegetarian dish, in addition to well-known avocado, carrot or cucumber versions, perhaps try roasted peppers with the balsamic dip.

WONDERING ABOUT THE ORIGINS OF SUSHI, I learn of several theories. Some tell of fish being pickled with rice in the fifth century BC. Some refer to it being brought in the fourth century BC by Buddhist priests returning from training in China, where rice was being cultivated. A master chef tells of how fish preserved in rice was sent to the land-bound then capital of Kyoto as a form of tax payment, forming early sushi, or nare zushi. It seems taxes are inescapable in all periods of history.

Whilst in Japan, my friend Hinesh gave a shapshot of the arduous training of a master chef he encountered. Beginning as a young teenager when he would accompany his senior chef, his *oyaji* (honourable father), to the local fish market as a bag carrier. Here, attentively witnessing the buying of fresh fish, he learned invaluable lessons. His job back at the store was to clean the day's bounty until it was spotless. Though he was not allowed near the counter where the sushi was prepared until several years of training had passed, he would watch from a respectful distance. One day he was finally granted the privilege of standing beside his master at the counter, fanning and cooling the steaming rice. He remembers the day fondly.

I am told that the nigiri sushi we know today was invented by Hanya Yohei as a nineteenth-century fast food, able to be eaten as a roadside snack, and not fermented like earlier varieties.

Cajun Spice Beer Butter Prawns with Sourdough

SERVES 4

3 tbsp butter

1 garlic clove, crushed

1 tbsp Cajun spice blend

8 tbsp beer (120ml)

1 tbsp double cream

12 large raw king prawns,
   in their shells

chopped fresh coriander,
   to serve

sourdough bread, to serve

This is inspired by a dish at Bubba Gump's on the Santa Monica Pier and will always taste of the warmest LA evenings to me. It was one of those brief, oh so lucky times when everything feels right in your world, and when time, in a rare gesture of kindness, stops for a moment so you can breathe life in. I was so relaxed, enjoying banter with the waiting staff, watching the seagulls and licking the sublime sauce from my fingers, that I completely forgot to ask for the recipe.

Until I return there, this is how I shall continue to make them at home, poured into a large bowl into which everyone reaches, dunking their pieces of bread. Of course, you can also serve it in individual bowls if you are not keen on being quite so familiar with your fellow diners.

I love using sourdough bread with this, which I first tried at the Boudin Bakery in San Francisco, with ladlefuls of the creamiest chowder, eaten while we huddled from the surprising August winds that are so sharply chill they go straight through you, freezing your bones in an instant.

Melt the butter in a pan over a very low heat. Add the garlic, fry for 1 minute and then add the Cajun spice, a few grindings of black pepper and a sprinkling of sea salt to taste. Stir in 4 tablespoons of the beer along with the cream, then add the prawns. Stir well to coat and turn up the heat a little, allowing the mixture to bubble, and cook the prawns for a few minutes until pink.

Serve in individual bowls or in a large sharing bowl in the centre of the table with another tablespoon of beer poured over the top for each of the 4 guests. Finally, scatter over some chopped coriander. Serve with sourdough bread to dunk and mop up the juices.

Use piri piri or cayenne instead of Cajun spice if you like. For a dry version without sauce, just fry the prawns in a non-stick pan with butter (perhaps a flavoured one) and then splash with a little beer and cook till the shells are golden brown and the flesh pink.

Arancini with Green Pepper and Green Chilli Butter

Arancini are fried balls of risotto rice, whose Italian name means 'little oranges'. You can, of course, make and cool a plain risotto if you wish to make a large batch of these to share for a gathering or party but I have always made these bites with leftover risotto, and I frequently don't share them with anyone at all.

Place the butter, green pepper, chilli and lime together in a blender and whiz to combine. Add some white pepper and salt to season then shape into a log in cling film and freeze until solid.

Divide the risotto rice into 16 and shape into balls. Cut a small chunk of the butter and press into the centre, shaping the rice around it to encase. Put the beaten egg and the breadcrumbs into separate shallow dishes and dip or brush the balls in egg then roll and coat in bread-crumbs. Fry in oil in a shallow pan until golden all over.

You could dip in plain flour instead of breadcrumbs. Perhaps, rather than stuff with butter, fry balls of plain risotto in garlic butter instead. Or mix some pesto, or citrus zest, into the butter and stuff with that.

MAKES ABOUT 16

100g salted butter, softened

25g / ¼ of a green pepper, sliced with no pith or seeds

¼ tsp finely chopped green chilli, deseeded

A generous squeeze of lime

White pepper and coarse salt to season

500g cold, cooked risotto

1 large egg, beaten

Breadcrumbs

Oil for frying, such as mild olive oil

Sweet Potato Mini Pasties

MAKES 28

1 tbsp vegetable oil

2 tsp black mustard seeds

2 shallots, finely chopped

1 garlic clove, finely chopped

1/2 tsp dried red chilli flakes

1/4 tsp turmeric

400g sweet potato, cooked and
  diced

1/4 tsp salt

2 tsp lemon juice

1 tbsp finely chopped coriander

4 sheets ready-rolled puff pastry
  (2 x 375g packets)

1 egg, beaten

These I make in a similar way to a batch of cupcakes – often in the afternoon, a pile of small savoury treats instead of sweet ones, with a cup of tea, or given away as an easily transported gift in a foil-wrapped heap. Mostly, I will make the filling first and leave to cool, coming back to encase spoonfuls in pastry some hours later. Although I have indicated the size of the cutter I use, you can make these any size you like. I like the lemon and spices, especially the peppery warmth when the black mustard seeds burst in the mouth, against the almost candied taste of the sweet potato. Serve with Greek yoghurt or crème fraîche, or some ketchup mixed with a little toasted cumin.

Heat the vegetable oil in a frying pan on a lowish heat and add the mustard seeds. Fry for about 30 seconds until they are sizzling, then add the shallots and garlic, cooking for a few minutes until softened. Stir in the chilli and turmeric. Add the sweet potato, stir well to mix with the spices, turn the heat up and cook for a couple more minutes, stirring frequently.

Put the mixture in a bowl and add the salt, lemon juice and coriander, gently stirring in. Leave to cool completely.

Preheat the oven to 200°C/Fan 180°C/Gas 6.

With each sheet, unroll the pastry on a floured surface and roll ever so slightly to soften and make smooth. It should be around 3mm thick. Using a 7.5-cm cutter, cut out 10 discs from a sheet of pastry. Gather up the pastry edges and leftovers into a ball and roll out flat, cut out another 3 discs, roll leftovers together again and cut out another 1. This should give you 14 discs to make 7 pasties from each sheet of pastry.

Mix the egg with 1 tablespoon of water to create an egg wash and brush round the edge of each disc. Carefully place about 2 tablespoons of mixture in the centre of a disc. Take another disc and place it gently on the top. The filling may try to escape. Just pull away any stray bits of filling, adding back into the bowl, then seal the edges with a fork, pressing and crimping all the way round to create a border.

Lift the pasties gently, using a palette knife so as not to tear them, placing onto a greased baking tray. Brush the tops and sides with egg wash and bake for about 12–15 minutes or until golden and well risen.

Use other vegetables if you like, such as regular potato, or perhaps the mashed innards of an aubergine roasted in its skin. Maybe you would like to use different pastry and make filo parcels or make ricepaper spring-rolls.

Ginger Chicken Soup with Lemon and Artichoke

SERVES 6

2 tbsp olive oil

1 tbsp butter

1 large onion, chopped

2 bay leaves

2 garlic cloves, halved lengthways

2 carrots, halved lengthways

1 leek, cut into chunks

2 sticks of celery, cut into chunks

4 cloves

1.5 litres chicken stock

500g chicken breast

1 whole baby globe artichoke

a piece of fresh ginger, roughly
   2cm x 3cm, peeled and cut
   into thin slices

2 preserved lemons, pips
   removed, finely chopped

good pinch of ground ginger

Greek yoghurt and chopped
   flat-leaf parsley, to serve

My local butchers are on fine form one astringent morning, tucking free chicken bones for stock into the bag with my meat, advising me to roast them well before boiling them up. We speak fondly for a while about the delicious 'Jewish penicillin' and matzo balls we have tried in St John's Wood. As I feel a cold persevering, a fortifying chicken soup sounds a good idea, and ginger might be a useful addition.

They cook ginger chicken soup in Zanzibar too; the Arabs carried ginger there in the thirteenth and fourteenth centuries on trade routes. I am reassured by their similar pairing of flavours, but I will add salty preserved lemons and the succulent leaves of baby artichoke to my soup too.

Heat the olive oil and butter then fry the onion until soft. Add the bay leaves, garlic, carrots, leek, celery and cloves and season with salt and pepper. Pour in the stock, bring to the boil, add the chicken breasts and simmer for 25 minutes.

Meanwhile, boil the artichoke in plenty of well-salted water for 30 minutes. Remove and set upside-down to drain.

Strain the stock, set the chicken aside and shred with a fork.

Reheat the stock, adding the slices of ginger, preserved lemon and ground ginger. Bring to the boil, reduce to a simmer and add the shredded chicken and artichoke leaves to heat through: about 5 minutes. Serve topped with a dollop of Greek yoghurt and some chopped parsley. Refrigerate any leftover artichoke and have it with salad the next day.

This is also excellent with silky pieces of tofu instead of chicken.

FIVE THOUSAND YEARS AGO GINGER was regarded as an almost mystical cure-all by the Chinese and Indians. This antler-like 'horn root', as named in ancient Sanskrit, was traditionally treated more as medicine than the flavouring I have come to rely upon so faithfully. Later, the Romans used ginger from India widely but, as the empire fell, it too fell out of favour. It is claimed to have been rescued by Marco Polo's travels to the East, its monetary value soaring. But it is the palm-fringed island of Jamaica that provides most of the world's ginger today, the root having been introduced to the Caribbean via sixteenth-century ships. Even Queen Elizabeth I could not resist its rich warmth: she is credited with using the dried, powdered spice to invent the popular gingerbread man. I cannot quite imagine her rolling up her frill-cuffed sleeves though.

Gin and Herb Broth

SERVES 4–6

1 tbsp olive oil

3 sticks of celery, thinly sliced

1 garlic clove, sliced

1 litre vegetable stock

2 slices of fresh ginger

1 slice of lime

8 peppercorns

4 tbsp gin

1 sprig of thyme

3 sprigs of lemon thyme

4 sprigs of flat-leaf parsley finely chopped, including stalks

2 basil leaves, finely chopped

2 mint leaves, finely chopped

2 blades of chives, finely chopped

small handful fresh coriander, finely chopped, including stalks

It is only recently that I have been exploring the flavours of dashes of spirits, wines and liquors in foods, how they merge with and transform other ingredients in cooking and on the palate. Sometimes I create dishes out of curiosity, sometimes necessity, sometimes sheer mood. This soup came about when I was ill and had completely lost my appetite. I wanted something clear and clean, almost astringent and medicinal, to soothe my insides, and I was keen on the idea of having a transparent broth, in the manner of Thai Tom Yum soup, but steeped with a jumble of health-giving fresh herbs. Because the quantities are so minute, this really is something to make with leftover herbs from the fridge or freezer, and not to buy herbs specially for. I like the slightly numbing and lulling edge of the juniper gin (white wine I felt would be too sweet, I wanted something more savoury) with the nursing antiseptic of the ginger and the cleansing celery. I am aware that I am not making this sound very appealing, but if you try it you will understand. Serve in a small bowl with chunks of warm, fresh white bread to mop it up or, better still, use the liquid to gently poach fish.

Heat the oil in a saucepan and add the celery and garlic. Fry for about a minute, then add the stock, ginger, lime and peppercorns and season with salt. Simmer for 10 minutes then turn the heat down very low and add the gin and herbs. Stir, heat for a minute then turn the heat off and allow to steep for 10 minutes before serving.

I like the flavour of coriander to dominate, but you can play with the ratios to highlight your own favourite herb. You could also try this using the more liquorice or aniseed herbs, such as tarragon and chervil, perhaps even adding a star anise. Or you may like to dispense with some of the herbs, choosing just one and replacing the others with some shredded spinach, cabbage or pak choi. Alternatively, you could add very finely chopped leeks, using perhaps just thyme, and simmering gently until cooked before adding the gin.

Chilled Macadamia and Black Olive Soup

I must admit this cold soup resulted from an oversight on my part. I had intended to make ajo blanco, a popular Spanish chilled almond soup, in small ice-frosted cups for a summer gathering, but upon returning home I realised I had forgotten the almonds and there was no time to venture out again. I had a bag of macadamias in the cupboard and so it was made with those, reducing the usual amount of garlic to balance with such a mild nuttiness and thinning it out a little more than usual. I like the blanket of creamy paleness spiked by a few salty, smooth raven-hued olives.

Tear the bread up roughly into big pieces and place in a large bowl with the macadamia nuts. Pour in a little milk, just enough to moisten all the bread, using your hands to check, and mix to make sure all the bread and nuts are coated in milk. Cover and leave to soak for an hour to soften the nuts.

Squeeze the milk out of the bread and place the bread in a food processor with the nuts and garlic. While blending, add the oil, and then the water, slowly, bit by bit. Finally, add the sherry. Chill until cold. Serve scattered with a few black olives.

This is a lovely way to use up stale bread, with just some nuts and olives from the pantry. Perhaps try cashews instead, or even brazil nuts with crisp-fried bacon or pancetta.

SERVES 4–6

175g day-old good quality white bread, with crusts removed
200g macadamia nuts
milk, to moisten the bread
2 garlic cloves
175ml extra virgin olive oil
700ml water
about 6 black olives per person
2 tbsp sherry

Tiger Prawn and Mandarin Soup

SERVES 4

2 shallots, finely chopped

1 large red chilli, finely chopped (remove the seeds if you don't like too much heat)

1 garlic clove, finely chopped

about 8 sprigs of fresh coriander, finely chopped, including stalks

1 tsp grated fresh ginger

1 tsp soft brown sugar

1 tsp vegetable oil

400ml can of coconut milk

400ml chicken stock

1 tbsp fish sauce

1 star anise

200g raw, peeled king prawn tails

300g can of mandarin segments in natural juice

a couple of handfuls of spinach, finely shredded

lime wedges, to serve

This soup is perfect for soothing frayed nerves and generally cheering oneself up. There is something about the clearing heat of the chilli, the sumptuousness of the prawns, the leafy goodness of the spinach, the exotic creaminess of the coconut and the surprise of the juicy mandarin that lifts the spirits. It's also very easy to make on short notice, most of the ingredients being those you might have kicking about, leaving only the prawns to pick up. Luxurious yet honest and balanced, this is a bowl of aromatic reassurance.

Crush together the shallots, chilli, garlic, coriander, ginger and sugar in a mortar with a pestle. Heat the oil in a large pan and add the crushed spice mixture. Stir-fry for 1 1/2 minutes on not too high a heat, just below medium, then add the coconut milk, stock, fish sauce and star anise. Cook gently on a low heat for 10 minutes.

Stir in the prawns and simmer for 2 minutes. Add about 20 mandarin segments (keep the remainder and their juice for another dish) and the spinach, stir very gently and switch off the heat. Serve immediately with lime wedges.

You could make this with chicken or with scallops, mackerel or whole prawns with their shells still on. Pak choi or another green leaf, such as kale or cabbage, would work too.

Roasted Carrot Soup with Nectarine and Red Pepper Salsa

SERVES 6–8

a quarter of a red onion, very finely chopped (I go over the chopped onion with a mezzaluna to cut it into very small pieces)

1/4 tsp fresh ginger juice (about a 4cm x 1cm piece, peeled and grated using a microplane over a small bowl, then take all the grated ginger, including the remains on top of the microplane, and squeeze to release the juice)

1/2 tsp lime juice

1/2 tsp rice vinegar

2 tsp caster sugar

2 tbsp olive oil

500g carrots

1 tbsp clear honey

1 tsp ground cumin

2 red peppers

2 tsp vegetable oil

3 tbsp butter

1 onion, chopped

1 tbsp plain flour

850ml vegetable stock

2 nectarines, diced

a few sprigs of coriander, finely chopped

I have some Chantenay carrots, their green tresses cascading out of my veg box. These are perfect for soup, with a small spoonful on top of something light, bright and peppy to lift it out of heavy starchiness. I prefer thinner, home-made carrot soups to the gloopy, monotonous, store-bought varieties, adding my own flavours. With their crisp sweetness, nectarines complement the carrots, along with some red peppers, roasted to intensify their flavour.

I dust the amber carrots with cumin to lend both earthiness and a lemony bite, which will mingle with a touch of honey to caramelise in the oven. To the roasted pepper and nectarine I will add a dash of fresh lime, ginger and coriander. Not much, just enough in the background to stop it all being too flatly sweet. However, a little white wine vinegar would not be a bad option either.

Preheat the oven to 190°C/Fan 170°C/Gas 5.

Combine the onion, ginger juice, lime juice, rice vinegar and caster sugar, season with salt and pepper, and set aside while you prepare the soup and peppers. This is the basis of the salsa.

Pour the olive oil into a roasting tin and heat in the oven for 5 minutes to get it nice and hot. Meanwhile, trim, scrub and dry the carrots. Add the carrots to the hot oil, drizzle with the honey and dust with the cumin. Toss everything in the pan to make sure the carrots are well coated. Brush the peppers with the vegetable oil and place on a baking tray. Put the carrots in the middle of the oven, with the peppers just underneath.

Roast the carrots for 20 minutes, tossing and swishing around the pan halfway through to coat the carrots in all the caramelised juices. Remove the carrots and let them cool, then chop into small chunks.

Roast the peppers for 40 minutes, turning them over halfway through. Place in a food bag and seal or put in a bowl and cover immediately with cling film. This is to steam the peppers, allowing them to slip easily out of their charred skins when cool.

Melt the butter in a large pan. Add the onion and cook for 5 minutes until softened. Briskly stir in the flour. Pour in the stock, stirring as you do so.

Add the carrots and season with a good grinding of pepper and some salt. Bring to the boil, cover and simmer for 10 minutes. Allow to cool slightly and then, using a hand-held or jug blender, whizz until smooth, adding extra boiling water to get to the consistency you like if it is too thick. I like mine a bit thinner and smoother than most, so I add a little water here.

Gently place the soft, moist peppers flat on the chopping board, make a slit lengthways along the skin and ease the skin away. Pull out and discard the core. Cut the flesh in half and remove the seeds. Put any pepper juices in a bowl to add to the salsa. Dice the flesh.

Add the peppers, and the pepper roasting juice, the nectarines and the coriander to the onion mixture. Reheat the soup then ladle it into bowls and top with a generous spoonful of the salsa.

If you like cumin, dry-roast a teaspoon of the seeds in a pan, bruise in a pestle and mortar and stir into the soup before ladling into bowls and topping with the salsa.

Pea and Lemongrass Soup

SERVES 6

2 tbsp olive oil

25g butter

1 large onion, chopped

1 garlic clove, chopped

4 stalks of lemongrass, finely chopped and then whizzed in processor, or use a knife or mezzaluna to create flakes

1 litre chicken stock

450g fresh or frozen peas

half a lime

a handful of coriander, chopped

In Norse mythology, it is said that Thor gave peas to humans as punishment. All the better for us.

My fresh peas deserve citrus and, handily, I have some chopped lemongrass in the freezer, which will go nicely. Frozen peas are absolutely an option too, and I would use them if I didn't already have these pods sat before me, plump and taut in a colander, like mischievous children bursting with secrets.

Heat the oil and butter together in a large pan. When the butter has melted, add the onion and garlic and cook gently for 5 minutes. Stir in the lemongrass, then pour in the stock. Bring to the boil, then simmer for 10 minutes. Add the peas and simmer for a further 3 minutes. Cool slightly, then using a hand-held or jug blender, whizz till smooth. Serve with a good squeeze of lime and the coriander.

You might like to try a pea soup with lime zest and juice, or perhaps, taking a lead from the Japanese, add some wasabi. A plain pea soup topped with a few crumbled pieces of goat's cheese and a drizzle of basil oil is also quite nice.

Sweet Basil Pesto

Although it takes time, and some effort, you get the perfect rustic texture when you pound a pesto properly using a pestle and mortar rather than pulverise it in a food processor. Indeed, that is what the name 'pesto' means – to pound (from *pestare*). I picked up some stalks of sweet basil at a Thai store for this. Holy basil is generally best for cooking, such as adding to stir-fries, but I love this sweet basil version, with its slightly mintier taste than regular basil pesto. A shimmering blanket of bruised leaves which goes particularly well with fat cushions of gnocchi, freshly bought from an Italian deli.

Pound the garlic and basil leaves together with a few pinches of coarse salt, then add the pine nuts and Parmesan, pounding as you go, and gradually adding the olive oil.

Varieties of pesto are well-known and popular. In supermarkets and at food fairs I have tried all sorts, from walnut to cashew and coriander to sun-dried tomato to parsley. Try using combinations of herbs and nuts with the oil and Parmesan as you wish. I also like pesto smeared on flatbreads and used as a base for the thinnest crispy pizzas.

SERVES 4

1 garlic clove
2 handfuls of Thai sweet basil leaves, about 25g
coarse salt
75g pine nuts, very lightly toasted
20g Parmesan, grated
8 tbsp mild olive oil

Pasta with Walnuts and Chilli

SERVES 4

1 tbsp walnut oil

1 onion, chopped

2 garlic cloves, chopped

125g walnut pieces

a handful of fresh coriander

1 tsp crushed chillies in oil (I'm
   using piri piri)

pasta of your choice, about 100g
   per person

butter, natural yoghurt and sea
   salt, to serve

This is an adaptation of a recipe from a dear friend from long, long ago when I was a young student, far away from home and without its comfort. My best friend's mother, Sabiha, was a natural and excellent cook of the very best kind: ever learning, absorbing, evolving, generous. And, after my mum, the first person whose food I came to crave, a taste of familial warmth stolen from a stream of wholesome foil packages. The first meal she cooked for me was a Thai green curry, its aromatic vapours suddenly filling the room in moments, as delicate and dream-like as those carefree days of my youth, gradually dissipating with time.

Her recipes taught me a great deal, and I sometimes adapt them to suit what's in my store cupboard. This pesto-like mixture is usually made with raw onions and garlic, (but I cook them for a more mellow flavour) and is traditionally eaten with a delicate pastry, forming a dish called prappu, eaten in the mountainous, rugged landscapes of Asia. I like to eat this with pasta such as linguine, adding a little creamy yoghurt.

Heat the oil in a frying pan and fry the onion and garlic until soft, then add the walnuts and fry for a couple more minutes. Put all of this into a food processor with a good handful of coriander and pulse to a coarse paste. Stir in the chillies. I then toss spoonfuls of this with hot, buttered pasta and add a dollop of natural yoghurt and a sprinkling of sea salt.

I use a teaspoon of piri piri (lots of places sell this, and other chillies in oil), because I like this quite hot, plus I like its tanginess, but if you don't like so much heat, use half a teaspoon. Or you could use some fresh red chilli instead, as much as you like for your own heat preference, and maybe add a dash of lemon juice to the mixture too. You could use crème fraîche instead of yoghurt to stir in at the end. And cashews would work nicely for a paste like this, as would almonds. Try using mint or parsley instead of coriander, maybe with a touch of harissa. Perhaps some cashews with a drop of lime and a touch of galangal stir-fry spice paste? Or stick to the walnuts but mix them with sun-dried tomato paste.

Buttermilk-soaked Chicken with Ciabatta, Butter Beans and Brazils

With a drop of sunshine, samba in my ear and this salad on the table, I feel like I am living and breathing summer. I cut and soak the chicken the night before, and you could also barbecue it until golden and just a touch charred instead of cooking it in a pan. I particularly like the grapefruit, which teases out the lemony undertones of the beautifully verdant basil oil and goes well with the jagged rocket. Toasted brazils are also a personal pleasure; their sturdy, smooth, satisfying snap between the molars enjoyed just as much here as when freshly dipped into melted chocolate. I am grateful to the Portuguese and Spanish for bringing them to Europe in the 1500s, these *almendras de los Andes* (almonds of the Andes).

SERVES 4

2 chicken breasts
150ml buttermilk
2 tbsp plain flour
olive oil, for frying
about 32 brazils, halved
4 thick slices of ciabatta, cut into chunks
410g can of butter beans, drained
rocket for 4 people
basil oil and grapefruit zest, to serve

Cut the chicken breasts in half horizontally, place in a large food bag and flatten with a rolling pin, bashing them out a bit. Pour the buttermilk into the bag, rubbing it into the chicken. Marinate in the fridge overnight or at least for a couple of hours.

Season the flour well with salt and white pepper. Wipe off the excess buttermilk then dust the chicken pieces in the flour. Heat some olive oil in a frying pan and fry the chicken over a medium heat for about 3–4 minutes on each side until deeply golden.

Remove the chicken from the pan and drain on kitchen paper, while adding the brazils and ciabatta to the hot oil and frying for about 3 minutes until lightly golden. Add the butter beans to warm through.

Cut the hot chicken into strips and add to a bowl of rocket with the ciabatta, brazils and butter beans from the pan. Toss well. Dress with a drizzle of basil oil and a generous grating of grapefruit zest.

Yoghurt is also widely known as wonderful for marinating meat. You could also use chickpeas or perhaps other beans and try toasting cubes of focaccia instead.

Grilled Goat's Cheese Salad with Hazelnuts, Pomegranate and a Blueberry Dressing

At the threshold of autumn, the air sparked with sharpness, I spy the last dusty-indigo blueberries of the season. I recall a Manhattan breakfast of perfect pillow pancakes and velvety, mellow fruitfulness. I make an inky, glossy dressing with mine – not sharp, not cloying, but with a soft fruitiness and jammy depth spiked with black pepper to cut through the richness of the goat's cheese. I like mild, fresh goat's cheeses, their newborn salty soapiness ringed with citrus, but for this dish I go for a rinded variety with a more mature flavour and texture that will withstand the heat of grilling, yielding only slightly in the centre. Buttery lamb's lettuce provides a clean, neutral foil for the cheese and dressing, and to add a bright top note of fresh sweetness, an early, blushing pomegranate is perfect.

Put the shallots in a pan with 1 tablespoon of the olive oil and the crushed garlic, stirring and frying for a minute, just to soften a little. Tumble in the blueberries, vinegar, sugar and a few grinds of black pepper. Stir and allow this mixture to gently stew on a very low heat for about 10 minutes. Then switch off the heat and let it cool.

Strain the mixture through a sieve into a bowl, pressing and pushing the solids with a wooden spoon to extract as much fruity liquid as possible. Don't discard the solids; refrigerate them in a covered container. Stir the remaining 2 tablespoons of olive oil into the blueberry liquid and add another grind of black pepper.

Put the goat's cheese, cut-side up, on greaseproof paper and place under a hot grill for 5 minutes. Or grill for just over a minute to warm up the whole cheese and then finish with a blast from a blowtorch until blemished to golden brown.

Meanwhile, toast the hazelnuts in a dry frying pan until golden.

Serve the cheese with the lamb's lettuce, pomegranate and hazelnuts and a good splash of the dressing.

The leftover garlicky blueberry solids are excellent served with hot or cold meats such as ham or roast beef, or spread in a Wensleydale sandwich, or used as a base layer for a savoury tart, or even added to some shredded duck in pancake wraps. With the goat's cheese, why not try raspberry and mint as flavours for the dressing next time, with rocket? Or a gooseberry or even a tamarind dressing, or perhaps an orange and cinnamon dressing with a salad of watercress and pine nuts.

SERVES 4

2 shallots, chopped
3 tbsp extra virgin olive oil
1 garlic clove, crushed
300g blueberries
1 tbsp red wine vinegar
20g soft dark brown sugar
2 rounds of goat's cheese, halved horizontally (use 4 rounds if for a main course)
40g whole blanched hazelnuts
a couple of handfuls of lamb's lettuce per person
4 tbsp pomegranate kernels

Clove Salt Beef with Figs, Watermelon Pepper Jelly and Radicchio

SERVES 4

650g ripe watermelon flesh, deseeded and chopped (I used a whole average-sized watermelon)

5 gelatine leaves

squeeze of lemon

260g sliced salt beef

olive oil, to drizzle

1/4 tsp ground cloves

4 fresh figs, quartered length-ways

enough radicchio for 4

green lettuce leaf of choice to mix with the radicchio

a few handfuls of black olives

3 tbsp extra virgin olive oil

1 tsp clear honey

Cracking open a watermelon is always faintly exciting. What a treasure it must have seemed in the Kalahari desert of Africa, where it was first harvested, up to a hundred melons on a single vine like jewelled charms on a chain, buried with Egyptian kings to quench them in the afterlife. I love how the savoury watermelon jelly cubes flit among this salad like gemstones, with the fragrant salt beef, so tender it falls apart at the mere proximity of a finger. The figs add regal sweetness, contrasted by the bitter and beautiful radicchio.

Prepare the jelly a good few hours in advance of eating the salad; better still, make it the day before.

Place the watermelon chunks in a food processor or blender and whizz till liquid. Sieve into a jug, pushing all the available juice out of the solids, to give about 500ml.

Either while doing this or just after, depending upon which type of gelatine you are using, soak the leaves of gelatine in cold water for either half an hour or 5 minutes if using the quick-dissolving variety. Then squeeze to remove excess water.

Heat the watermelon juice in a pan to boiling. Skim off any scum or foam. Leave to cool for 5 minutes, pour through a strainer and then whisk in the gelatine leaves. Continue to whisk for about 5 minutes until thoroughly dissolved. Add a squeeze of lemon.

Pour this into an ice-cube tray, coarsely grind some black pepper over each cube and chill for a couple of hours. Stir the pepper into the jelly a bit and then grind some more over the top. Chill until firmly set, another hour and a half at least. If mine still isn't set by the time I need it, I sometimes put it in the freezer for 15 minutes or so to speed it up.

Preheat the oven to 180°C/Fan 160°C/Gas 4.

Drizzle the salt beef with a little olive oil and rub in a bit. Then also rub a very small amount of ground cloves into the meat. Not a lot, as ground cloves are very strong, just a little picked up on an oil-moistened finger to give a hint of flavour. Wrap the meat in foil and place in the oven for 20 minutes to heat through nicely.

Quarter some jelly cubes and toss these with the quartered figs, the leaves and olives. Add the hot meat. Mix the extra virgin olive oil and honey together and then drizzle over the salad.

Perhaps use some torn gammon or roast beef with this salad instead of the salt beef. A cranberry jelly would also be quite nice with pepper, or use an entirely different jelly, such as Champagne or tomato.

Chickpea Fritters with Beetroot, Buffalo Mozzarella and Pink Pepper

2 raw beetroots, around the same size as a ball of mozzarella

410g can of cooked chickpeas, drained

100g plain flour, sifted

1 tsp baking powder, sifted

2 large eggs, separated

150ml milk

1 tbsp fresh coriander, finely chopped, plus extra to garnish

good squeeze of lemon juice

1 garlic clove, crushed

$\frac{1}{4}$ tsp cayenne pepper

1 tsp tahini

vegetable oil, for frying

4 tbsp salted butter

2 tsp pink peppercorns, crushed with a pestle and mortar

2 balls of buffalo mozzarella

The colours of this are just beautiful, particularly the rosy-hued pink pepper butter. However, the beetroot will bleed quickly so do make sure to plate it up only when you are ready to eat, or it may begin to look slightly gruesome. The chickpea fritters, crisp and nutty, are made with the popular flavours of hummus. The mozzarella, a fat pearl in the briny water, I cut it into milky, silky slabs, supporting the watery cleanliness of the beetroot, with the pepper adding contrast and polish.

Preheat the oven to 180°C/Fan 160°C/Gas 4.

First, cook the beetroot. Trim the stalks off, then wrap the beetroot in foil and bake for 1 hour until tender. Allow to cool.

Pulse the chickpeas a few times in a food processor until crushed.

Combine the flour and baking powder in a large bowl. Whisk the egg yolks and milk together in a separate bowl and then beat into the flour. Add the crushed chickpeas, coriander, lemon, garlic, cayenne and tahini, stirring, and season well with salt and pepper. Whisk the egg whites into soft peaks and then fold into the mixture.

Heat a centimetre of oil in a large frying pan over a medium heat. For each fritter, drop in a tablespoon of mixture, then top immediately with a second. Fry, in batches of about 3 at a time, for about 3–4 minutes on each side until golden and crisp. Drain and keep warm while making the rest.

Melt the butter with the pink peppercorns and let it sizzle slightly then switch off the heat. Slice the mozzarella. Peel the skin off the beetroot – using rubber gloves if you like so as not to stain your fingers – and slice it. Place a fritter on a plate, top with a slice of beetroot, then a slice of mozzarella, and then repeat. Drizzle the butter over the top and add a sprinkle of coriander. Serve immediately.

If you come across them, try golden or candy stripe beetroot. You could also use slices of cooked aubergine or sweet potato instead of the beetroot, or maybe large portabella mushrooms. Spice the butter with other flavourings, such as cracked coriander seed, or perhaps make a fresh garlic butter with parsley. You could also try making fritters with butter beans, flavouring them with rosemary.

Roast Acorn Squash with Pear and Kiwi Chutney

MAKES 850ML

FOR THE PEAR AND KIWI CHUTNEY

3 tbsp vegetable oil

2 tsp panch pooran spice mix

2 tsp coriander seeds, cracked
   with a pestle in mortar

4 cloves

half a large onion (about 100g),
   finely chopped

2 garlic cloves, finely chopped

1 tsp dried red chilli flakes

a piece of fresh ginger, about
   2cm x 3cm, sliced (I get about
   5 slices out of this)

200g light muscovado sugar

200ml white wine vinegar

2 tsp salt

8 pears (I use Packham), cored
   and cut into small chunks with
   the skins left on – squeeze
   some lemon juice over to
   prevent the flesh going brown
   while you fry the spices

4 large, ripe kiwi fruits, peeled
   and cut into small chunks

This dish is based on a very enjoyable starter served by super cook Hardeep Singh Kohli at a dinner party in early 2006. His version was butternut squash, served with a spicy Indian tomato chutney. I was struck by how well the squash, Parmesan (his slightly grilled) and chutney went together. I have chosen to make my chutney with Bengali panch pooran (a spice mix of fenugreek, nigella, black mustard, fennel and cumin), pear and kiwi.

Of the squashes I like acorn squash because of its more savoury flavour. Wholesome squash is thought to be the first food ever cultivated by indigenous Americans. The beautiful skins look like they have been stroked randomly with green paint, like an abstract painting. And I love the curve of the small quarters, roasting away in the oven like little sailboats.

Heat the oil in a large, heavy-based pan and add the panch pooran, coriander seeds and cloves. Fry for 2 minutes, stirring, until sizzling, then add the onion and garlic and fry for another couple of minutes until softened. Add the chilli flakes, ginger, sugar, white wine vinegar and salt and stir well. Add the fruit and then bring the mixture to the boil, dissolving the sugar.

Reduce the heat and simmer gently for 1 hour and 15 minutes until thick and jammy, stirring occasionally. Set aside for 5 minutes, then spoon into sterilised jars. Cover immediately with the lids or waxed discs and leave to cool completely. Store in a cool, dark place to mature for a couple of weeks before eating, then refrigerate once opened.

Preheat the oven to 200°C/Fan 180°C/Gas 6.

Quarter the squash and scoop out the seeds. Drizzle with olive oil and roast for 35 minutes.

Place a few shavings of Parmesan on top and then a grind of pepper. Serve with a little of the sharp, hot, sour chutney.

Plum and tamarind might be a nice chutney combination or maybe you would like to eat this with a fresh salsa? Of course, use any type of squash you like if acorn squash isn't available or isn't your preference.

1 squash serves 4 as a starter or small portion
olive oil, to drizzle
Parmesan shavings, to serve

Chicken Cakes with Seaweed and Lime

MAKES 18

2 sheets of seaweed
500g chicken breast
1 garlic clove, chopped
1 red chilli, deseeded and
    chopped
1 tsp pickled ginger
a handful of fresh coriander,
    roughly chopped
zest of 2 limes and juice of 1
50g breadcrumbs
1 tsp fish sauce
oil for brushing (I use mild
    olive oil)

These are absolutely delicious juicy little patties, particularly if you like umami, salty and sour flavours. The pickled ginger adds a tart sharpness I like. They were inspired by some bite-size fish lollipops I came across in a Japanese store, coated in a seaweed-flecked batter. You could make them larger and serve them as chicken burgers in rolls instead, with ketchup, or perhaps even shape the mixture on to skewers like sheesh kebabs and grill or barbecue them. I also like serving them to people who think they don't, or wouldn't, like seaweed. They are always pleasantly surprised when I reveal, after a few mouthfuls, that the vital ingredient is the shiny, flaky sheets of sea vegetable.

Preheat the oven to 200°C/Fan 180°C/Gas 6.

Fold the seaweed sheets in half, then in half again. Snip across into thin strips but not totally to the end, and then snip across the other way over a bowl to make small squares.

Chop the chicken breasts into small pieces and pulse in a food processor with the garlic, chilli, pickled ginger and coriander.

Combine the chicken mixture with the lime zest and juice, seaweed, breadcrumbs and fish sauce, then season with salt and pepper. Shape into 18 small patties and place on an oiled baking tray. Brush with oil and cook for 10 minutes on each side or until golden brown.

Perhaps serve with some mayonnaise spiked with a little lime zest and juice and with some home-made, skin-on chips. You could break up any leftover patties with a fork and use the mixture to make spring rolls, dim sum, little filo parcels or even stuffed baked tomatoes. Try making the patties with fish or crab, too.

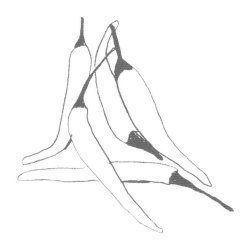

Paneer Rosemary Spears with Bitter Orange and Almond

I fell under the spell of rosemary some years ago now, adding sprigs of it to roast potatoes with cloves of garlic and sprinklings of coarse salt. I love its almost-bitter and pine-like quality, which I feel mirrors the bitterness of the orange zest. At the same time, it has a slightly lemon tone that picks out the citrus of the orange juice, both going well with the almonds.

Mix the almonds together with the orange zest, blossom water and juice, olive oil and some grinds of black pepper in a bowl. Add the paneer and, using your hands, gently toss with the almond mixture, then set aside.

Keeping the skin on, cut the potatoes into chunks roughly the same size as the paneer. Place in a pan, cover with cold water, bring to the boil and boil for about 4–5 minutes until cooked but not too soft. Drain and allow to cool.

Mix the marmalade with the olive oil until nice and supple.

Take a spear of rosemary and remove all the leaves from the part of the stalk that is firm and woody, leaving those on the tip. Slowly and very carefully thread on the paneer, potato and peppers alternately – gently so as not to cause a split in the paneer or vegetables. Depending upon the length of the rosemary, you should get two of each on each rosemary spear.

Place the threaded spears on a plate and gently but liberally brush with the marmalade mixture, rotating to make sure they are coated all over. Then take a little of the almond mixture and gently press on to each side of the chunks of paneer to coat.

Place the spears on an oiled baking sheet, using a strip of foil the exposed rosemary tails so they don't burn, then put under a hot grill and cook for about 2 minutes each side or until golden, gently and carefully rotating. The almond coating gets golden very quickly and needs watching carefully to make sure it doesn't catch.

Serve with natural yoghurt or crème fraîche infused with some torn rosemary leaves.

Try using the paste to encrust fish: place some fish fillets in a dish with a little white wine and rosemary sprigs, then press some of the paste on top of the fish. Or use with a rack or cutlets of lamb, or encrust a whole shoulder or leg and slow-bake. Rosemary, black pepper and orange would be fine with salty feta or halloumi but the delicate almond and orange-blossom water flavours will get lost with big pieces of intense cheeses, and will completely change the flavour balance.

MAKES 16

50g ground almonds
zest of 2 oranges
2 tsp orange-blossom water
2 tsp orange juice
2 tsp mild olive oil
227g block of paneer, cut into chunks of 2cm x 2cm
2 redskin potatoes, scrubbed
2 tbsp bitter orange or Seville orange marmalade
2 tsp mild olive oil
1 large orange pepper, cut into chunks roughly the same size as the paneer
16 rosemary spears
natural yoghurt or crème fraîche, to serve

IN THE
MIDDLE

In this section you'll find the dishes I think of as main meals, from anytime staples like effortless Foil-baked Feta to be scooped up in front of the television with warm crusty bread after a hard day at work to a meltingly soft Leg of Lamb with a Black Cherry, Tamarind and Walnut sauce you and your dinner guests can enjoy with a special bottle of wine and the golden flickers of candlelight.

There are dishes you can cook on the hob in just one pan, some of them in a flash, like the Piri Piri and Cocoa-rubbed steak or the Sumac Lamb Cutlets. Other times, I like to pop the ingredients in the oven and leave them to transform slowly over time whilst I get on with other things, like with the Rioja Pot Roast Chicken. Whether you fancy something light and fresh like a wedge of savoury tart with salad or some grilled fish or prefer a warming and comforting pie when the cold nights begin to creep in, this is where you'll find the recipes for your main lunch and supper dishes.

ON THE HOB

Wafer-sliced Duck Risotto with Spiced Plums and
Star Anise
Piri Piri and Cocoa-rubbed Steak
Sumac Cutlets with Rosehip Gravy
Brussels Sprouts with Ginger, Garlic and Soy
Rainbow Trout in an Oatmeal Crust with Poppy
Seed and Ginger Butter Sauce
Chicken with Pepperdew, Pineapple and Cashews

LIGHT AND FRESH

Tomato and Cumin Seed Tart
Lemon Sole with Julienne Ratatouille
Lime-seared Tuna
Sea Bass with Apple and Mint
Glass Noodles with Radish, Celery, Cucumber
and Dill
Chestnut, Chorizo and New Potato Tart
Spaghetti with Edamame and Pecorino

WARMING AND COMFORTING

Keema, Chilli and Coriander Pie
Baked Aubergine Crumbles with Sichuan Pepper
Garlic, Herb and Coriander Seed Turkey in Potatoes
Chicory and Wasabi Bake
Chilli Caramel Salmon Pie
Crumbled Lincolnshire Sausage, Cranberry, Olive
and Lemon Pasta
Baked Sausages with Tomato, Balsamic and Cumin
Baked Haddock with Spiced Breadcrumbs and Gobi
Plum and Coriander Ribs
Lapsang Souchong-scented Salmon with Nutmeg
Butter and Kale

SLOWLY IN THE OVEN

Rioja Chicken with Polenta Cakes
Leg of Lamb with Black Cherries, Tamarind and
Walnut
Roasted Onions with Pear Juice, Dijon Mustard
and Mozzarella
Garam Masala Chicken with Basil Couscous
Beef Stewed with Miso, Barley and Sun-kissed
Tomatoes
Confit of Duck Leg with Pine Nut Couscous and
Date Chutney

FOR ANY TIME

Steamed Hoki with Crushed Coriander and Crispy
Onions
Baked Monkfish with Harissa and Parma Ham
Foil-baked Feta
Saffron Quails Stuffed with Ricotta, Garlic and
Gooseberry Mash
Pork with Green Peppercorns, Water Chestnuts
and Lemon
Drumsticks with Sesame, Five-Spice and Coca-Cola
Upside-down Spiced Butter Chicken
Red-Grape Poussins with Fig, Hazlenut and Feta
Stuffing
Roasted Vegetables with Agave, Pineapple and Mint
Gremolata Rack of Lamb with Aduki Beans and
Frozen Lassi

FROM THE GRILL AND GRIDDLE

Red Snapper Brushed with Chipotle, Strawberry
and Rosé
Seared Mushrooms with Red Chilli Thari
Asparagus with Mustard Seed Cream
Courgettes Stuffed with Coffee Rice and Oregano
Paprika and Parmesan Chicken Skewers
Mirin Mackerel with Brown Rice and Spring Onion
Grilled Sardines with Beetroot, Pink Grapefruit and
Parsley

Wafer-sliced Duck Risotto with Spiced Plums and Star Anise

SERVES 4

4 duck breasts (skins on)

SPICED PLUMS AND
STAR ANISE SAUCE
4 ripe red plums, stoned, cut
 into small chunks
200ml red wine (I use a spicy
 Shiraz)
1 tbsp red wine vinegar
3 star anise
pared zest of 1 lemon
1 stick of cinnamon
1 tsp soft dark brown sugar

FOR THE RISOTTO
2 tbsp olive oil
1 tbsp butter
1 onion, finely chopped
1 garlic clove, finely chopped
1 litre lamb stock
300g arborio risotto rice
3–4 tbsp flat-leaf parsley,
 roughly chopped
250ml white wine
a little oil for frying (I use mild
 olive)

Biting into the acidity of raw plum skin can make me shudder, so I like this way of using the fruit, mellowed through cooking. Star anise sits well with plum, both of them enjoying a long history in China. They work their magic with soft strips of richly flavoured duck and, in a creamy variation on the sticky rice they might be eaten with in the East, I love them with a plate of the simplest, gentlest of risottos to warm me through.

Preheat the oven to 200°C/Fan 180°C/Gas 6.

Place all the ingredients for the spiced plums and star anise sauce together in a pan, partly cover and simmer very gently for 20 minutes. Switch off the heat, remove the lemon zest, add some black pepper and place to one side.

Season the duck breasts and then place skin-side down in a hot oven-proof frying pan with a tiny bit of oil. Fry for 5 minutes, then pour out the excess fat. Fry for another 5 minutes, then roast in the oven for 10 minutes. Switch the oven off, turn the duck skin-side up and leave to rest.

For the risotto, heat the olive oil and butter in large pan and, when the butter is foaming, add the onion and garlic and cook on a very low heat for about 5 minutes to soften. Heat the stock in a separate pan and keep it simmering away. Add the rice to the onions and garlic, turn up the heat and stir constantly. Pour in the wine straight away. Keep stirring until evaporated.

Over a low heat, add the stock a ladleful at a time, stirring and allowing each amount to fully absorb before adding another. This should take about 25 minutes. The rice should be plump and fluffy but still have a little bite at the centre of each grain. Take the risotto off the heat and allow to rest briefly, covered with a lid.

Slice the duck very thinly and serve on top of the risotto, adding the sauce at the final moment.

You could use dark cherries instead of plums, or go for a completely savoury version, maybe with diced aubergine and star anise.

PLUMS FEATURED in the literature of Confucius, dating all the way back to 479 BC. It was Pompey the Great who unveiled their charms to Rome, and another Great, Alexander, who spread them further to the Mediterranean.

Piri Piri- and Cocoa-rubbed Steak

PER PERSON
¼ tsp piri piri (crushed chillies in oil)
½ tsp cocoa
¼ tsp mild olive oil
¼ tsp maple syrup
pinch of salt
1 fillet steak
olive oil, for frying

For this, I use my favourite Portuguese piri piri chillies – a bottle of which I am never without. I think of it as freshly crushed fire, and am not sure I could ever live without it now, shameless addict that I am.

You might have heard of the Mexican concoction *mole*, which often uses chocolate in a savoury, chilli-enhanced meat dish. I thought I might try rubbing cocoa and feisty chilli together into a steak to marinate it, to give just a hint of chocolate but without the sauce. The partnership should be pleasing, given that both chocolate and chilli trigger the body to release endorphins. I enjoy mine best with golden, skin-on, freshly made chips and a crisp green salad.

Mix together the chilli, cocoa, olive oil, maple syrup and salt into a paste. Rub into the steak well and set aside to marinate at room temperature for 30 minutes.

Heat a little oil in a pan and fry the steak for a minute and a half on each side or to your liking.

Lime zest or finely chopped mint leaves might be another option. If you can't get piri piri, use another chilli in oil, or even chilli powder. Or take inspiration from the Mayans and add orange zest instead of chilli.

Sumac Cutlets with Rosehip Gravy

SERVES 2
4 lamb cutlets
olive oil, for drizzling, plus 1 tbsp for frying
1 tsp ground sumac
1 tbsp dried rosehip tea
half a lamb stock cube
knob of butter
½ tsp plain flour

Ground from the sour and astringent burgundy berries that originate in Iran and the southern Mediterranean, Sumac is a red earth-like powder that I often add to baked tomatoes, stews, or mix with yoghurt and thyme to make Lebanese labne, or rub with butter on to hot flatbreads with blackened edges.

Rosehip cordial, along with gripe water, was a flavour of my infancy. But despite being an extraordinary source of vitamin C and antioxidants, and a cooling tonic, rosehips sadly seem to have disappeared from today's jellies and jams. In this dish, I infuse my gravy with the fragrant romance of rosehips, gorgeous drizzled over crisp roast potatoes.

Drizzle the cutlets with olive oil and rub in the sumac. Leave to marinate at room temperature for 30 minutes.

Mix the rosehip tea with 3 tbsp boiling water and leave to steep for 5 minutes. Then pour this paste into a pan with 120ml water, the half stock cube and a knob of butter. Bring to the boil, boil for 1 minute, then turn the heat down to very low. Stir in the plain flour, stirring briskly to mix in well. Cook on a low heat for 1 minute, then strain.

Heat 1 tablespoon of olive oil in a frying pan over a high heat. Add the cutlets and fry for 2–3 minutes on each side for medium-rare. Allow to rest for a few minutes before serving with the rosehip gravy.

Follow the lead of Lebanese labne and mix sumac with yoghurt and dried thyme, marinating meat in this mixture before roasting or barbecuing. Try infusing gravies with other fruit teas, such as blackcurrant, hibiscus or raspberry, maybe adding a little chopped mint, too.

Brussels Sprouts with Ginger, Garlic and Soy

I prefer sprouts a little crunchy, not soggy and waterlogged. I cook other greens this way, such as pak choi or spinach, often tossing with noodles. They work well with the Chinese flavours here, the soy sauce reducing any bitterness. I serve them with wholewheat soba noodles or quinoa.

Writing this reminds me of my surprise upon eating the best Chinese food I had ever tasted some years ago in Ghana. Unlike the Cantonese food I had come across before, this was more like Sichuan cooking, although I suspect the Ghanaians, who always have a pot of oily chilli at the table, had added their own flavours. Their dishes, jollof rice in particular, made me feel at home, spiced as they were with the familiar powders of India, caught like butterflies as they passed by over Africa.

Heat the oil in a pan, add the garlic and ginger and stir-fry briskly until the garlic is just beginning to colour, then add the sprouts and stir-fry for about 3 minutes, finishing with a splash of soy sauce.

Perhaps try stir-frying the sprouts with diced pancetta and a splash of balsamic, or roast in a dish with a little cream and topped with breadcrumbs, perhaps also a little rosemary.

SERVES 2

1 tbsp toasted sesame oil
1 garlic clove, crushed
a piece of fresh ginger, about 4cm x 3cm, cut into thin strips
300g sprouts, halved lengthways (I like to use button sprouts, which are baby sprouts, but you can use small ordinary sprouts instead)
splash of soy sauce

Rainbow Trout in an Oatmeal Crust with Poppy Seed and Ginger Butter Sauce

SERVES 2

plain flour, for coating

1 egg, beaten

medium oatmeal, for coating

2 rainbow trout fillets, about 200g, skinned, washed, patted dry and cut into 4 long pieces

oil, for frying

2 tbsp butter

2 tsp poppy seeds

4 tbsp double cream

1 tsp grated fresh ginger

1/2 tsp ground ginger

I would hate for my kitchen to be without oats. With their heartening wholesomeness, they have often been overlooked and underrated in the past, but they have become an invaluable addition to my cupboard over the last five years. They are excellent for the digestive system and, like the Scots, I have come to think of them as nothing short of a superfood. But there is more to them than just spluttering panfuls of porridge, served with jam or trickles of honey. In this recipe, they are used in the place of breadcrumbs and treated to a drizzle of luxurious sauce, which I think they fully deserve.

Place the flour, egg and oatmeal on separate plates ready for dipping. Dip the strips of fish first into the flour, then the egg and then finally the oatmeal, patting to make sure they are evenly coated.

Pour about 1 cm of oil into a large frying pan to shallow-fry, and heat. When hot, add the fish slices and fry for about 4 minutes on each side until golden.

Heat the butter in a pan on a very low heat and add the poppy seeds. After a few seconds, when they are sizzling, whisk in the cream and fresh and ground ginger, season with salt and white pepper, and heat through. Serve the fish with the sauce and a vegetable such as green beans or spinach.

Although good for coating fish (mackerel is another good choice), you could also use an oat crust for chicken strips, with a lemon-thyme butter sauce with plenty of black pepper. Or even strips of steak, served with a creamy peppercorn sauce

Chicken with Pepperdew, Pineapple and Cashews

Torn between making a chicken tagine or sweet and sour, I decided to take elements from both and combine them in one dish. The base of this recipe is quite Moroccan, with cinnamon, ground ginger and coriander releasing their intoxicating perfume into the caramelised onion and tomato, then the final stage adds a sweet and sour vibrancy, with slightly hot and tart pepperdews contrasted with juicy pineapple. The cashews add much needed savoury bite and the coriander leaves provide freshness and a bridge for both sets of flavourings.

Heat the oil in a pan, add the onion and fry until soft and just turning golden brown. Add the garlic, cinnamon, ginger and coriander, season with salt and black pepper and cook for 1 minute with a splash of water. Add the tomatoes and cook on a low heat for 5 minutes, adding splashes of water so it doesn't get too dry. Then add the chicken, turn up the heat and stir-fry for 2–3 minutes. Make sure the chicken is well coated. Add the pepperdews, lime leaves and a squeeze of lemon and stir together. Pour in the chicken stock, bring to the boil, cover and gently simmer for 20 minutes, stirring occasionally. I put a cup of rinsed white basmati rice in a pan with 2 cups of water, a few slices of lime and a handful of green beans, topped and tailed and snipped in half widthways. Stir, bring to the boil, cover and steam on a very low heat for about 10–15 minutes.

Add the cashews, pineapple and coriander to the chicken, stirring in and heating through for a minute before serving. Serve with white basmati rice steamed with green beans and lime.

You could use fresh chunks of mango instead of pineapple, with slices of fresh red or green chilli. An adventurous twist would be not-too-ripe banana or plantain instead of the pineapple, with matchsticks of fresh ginger.

SERVES 4

1 tbsp oil
1 onion, chopped
1 garlic clove, crushed
$1/4$ tsp ground cinnamon
$1/4$ tsp ground ginger
$1/2$ tsp ground coriander
4 tbsp canned chopped tomatoes
400g chicken breast, diced
10 pepperdew peppers, cut into strips
2 lime leaves
1 lemon
375ml chicken stock
100g cashew nuts
130g fresh pineapple chunks or drained flesh from a 300g can
a handful of fresh coriander, chopped
basmati rice for 4
lime slices
a handful of green beans, if you have them

Tomato and Cumin Seed Tart

SERVES 4

1 tbsp olive oil, plus extra for greasing

1 tbsp butter

1½ tsp white wine vinegar

1 tsp caster sugar

3 pinches English mustard powder

2 tbsp double cream

2 tsp cumin seeds

tomatoes, whichever variety you like (I used 4 different coloured tomatoes and a handful of cherry tomatoes), small ones halved, large ones sliced

375g ready-rolled puff pastry

1 egg, beaten with a splash of water

50g Parmesan, grated

The first time I properly tasted a tomato was at a stall in a small town near Tuscany in 2005. In the telling manner of those who have a relationship with the produce they sell, I was warmly invited to sample one. Plucked from the vine with a sharp snap, a glowing orb was placed in my palm. Oh, so this is what tomato is supposed to taste like, I thought. For all those I have tasted before must surely have been ghostly illusions, picked before their time, leaving a pale, weeping, warehouse-refrigerator acidity haunting my palate. While these, well, these were firmly in the grip of life. For the first time, I actually believed the tomato was a fruit, irrefutable here in all its rude sweetness.

They say that chilli is addictive. I feel the same could be said for cumin. I find its smoky depths pretty irresistible. I like it very much here as I think it balances the sugar of the tomatoes, although I have also made versions studding the pastry with fennel seeds, which was perfectly fine. You need good, flavoursome tomatoes for this simple tart to come alive. Whether you plump for cherry, plum, heirloom, green or even yellow cherry tomatoes, the crucial thing is flavour.

Preheat the oven to 220°C/Fan 200°C/Gas 7. Place a baking sheet in there, towards the top, to heat up.

Meanwhile, heat the olive oil and butter in a frying pan. When the butter has melted, add the vinegar, sugar and mustard powder and cook for 1 minute, then add the cream, stir well, remove from the heat and set aside.

Toast the cumin seeds in a dry frying pan and set aside.

Lightly oil a second baking sheet and unroll the puff pastry sheet on to it. Prick all over the centre with a fork. Scatter the cumin seeds all over the pastry, including the sides and lightly press in. Using a sharp knife, score a line all round, about 1½ cm from the edge. Arrange the tomatoes within the line. Brush the pastry border with egg, then fold the edges in to meet the line and to create a folded border. Brush the border with egg again.

Drizzle the butter mixture over the tomatoes, scatter Parmesan on top and place the baking sheet on the hot baking sheet already in the oven (this is to help cook the base). Bake for 25–30 minutes until brown.

You might decide not to use the butter dressing but to spread a little pesto on the base instead.

Lemon Sole with Julienne Ratatouille

SERVES 4

half an aubergine (I use the thinner end at the top of the vegetable), cut into thin batons just a little longer than the width of the sole fillet

1 courgette, cut into long thin batons

half a red onion, thinly sliced

half a green pepper, cut into long thin batons

1 lemon

2 plum tomatoes, halved, deseeded and cut into long thin batons

olive oil

1 garlic clove, halved

8 large lemon sole fillets, about 130g each, trimmed and skinned (I get my fishmonger to do this), washed and patted dry

a few splashes of white wine

tapenade (I quite like kalamata tapenade) and flat-leaf parsley, to serve

This is based on a dish by chef Simon Rimmer, which was so stunningly colourful it immediately caught my eye, and I have enjoyed it very much a number of times since. I have made mine with the flavours of a ratatouille and with just a drizzle of a white wine and tapenade sauce. It makes a very fresh meal, the vegetables still with a bit of bite to them and the delicate fish just steamed through. This is nice on its own, or you could serve it with some spinach, or salad, or, to make a more substantial meal, some creamed potato.

Preheat the oven to 180°C/Fan 160°C/Gas 4.

Blanch the aubergine, courgette, onion and pepper batons by bringing a pan of salted water to the boil, adding the vegetables, boiling for 2 minutes, then draining and immersing into ice-cold water. Toss in a little lemon juice. Brush a large sheet of foil (large enough to place the fillets on and have enough left over to fold into a pouch) with some olive oil, and rub with the cut sides of the garlic, leaving the pieces on the foil.

Lay the fillets on a board with the thinnest ends nearest to you. Place a bunch of assorted vegetable batons, including the tomatoes, on the thin end of each fillet and roll the fillet up. Place on the foil.

Pour a splash of white wine over the fish rolls, then season. Wrap the foil up to create a loose pouch. Fold another piece of foil over the pouch if it is gaping, so that no steam can escape. Bake for 8–10 minutes or until the fish is cooked through and opaque.

Gently heat a few tablespoons of tapenade with enough white wine to make a sauce consistency, adding a little finely chopped fresh flat-leaf parsley. Drizzle over the fish and serve.

You could use all sorts of julienned vegetables to stuff the fish, maybe a selection of greens, such as baby leeks and green beans, or perhaps just one vegetable. You could make a vinaigrette-based sauce to serve along-side. Another, richer, idea might be to wrap the sole round a bundle of baby asparagus, then wrap some Parma ham around the sole, and roast, allowing the ham to crisp, and serving with a light mustard cream sauce.

LIKE THE MORE ENLIGHTENED SAILORS in the 1800s, it is rare for me to be without limes. These fruits, originally from Southeast Asia, are a dependable staple in my kitchen. Millions of gallons of lime juice, cheaply imported from Jamaica, were drunk by them to conquer scurvy, leading to their nickname as 'limeys'. Columbus took limes from the Canary Islands to the island of Hispaniola in 1493, planting them in his settlement of Isabella. These were then taken to St Augustine in Florida by the Spanish conquistadores. I am glad, for without this there would be no key lime pie, which I adore.

Lime-seared Tuna

The lime juice and zest 'cook' the tuna a little, which means only the briefest griddling is required. This is perfect in summer, particularly if you are barbecuing. I like to serve it sliced with crushed Jersey Royal potatoes and watercress. It's also good stuffed into warm pitta with salad.

SERVES 2
white pepper
2 tuna steaks
zest of 1 lime and juice of half
oil, for frying

Dust a little white pepper on each side of the tuna steaks, then rub in the lime zest and juice. Leave for about 5 minutes, then fry on a hot griddle pan moistened with a little oil for about 1½ minutes on each side, or to your liking.

Perhaps use other citrus fruits, or even some sumac. Or maybe even marinate in a little red or white wine vinegar, or balsamic, with a touch of sugar. For a Bajan lilt, rub in a tiny touch of brown sugar too and carefully splash with a hint of rum.

Sea Bass with Apple and Mint

SERVES 2

olive oil

1 onion, finely diced

2 garlic cloves, finely chopped

1 tsp white wine vinegar

1/2 Granny Smith apple, cored, peeled and finely diced

a knob of butter

2 tbsp finely chopped mint

2 tbsp finely chopped flat-leaf parsley

2 whole sea bass, about 475g each, cleaned, scaled and gutted, but left whole

350g new potatoes, scrubbed and diced

2 tbsp semolina

1 stalk of lemongrass

6 tbsp crème fraîche

chopped flat-leaf parsley, to serve

This is full of light flavours and a very good supper for a balmy evening, especially with the lemongrass crème fraîche. The thing I find with lemongrass is that it is best to prepare it right at the last minute. If you buy the stalks from the supermarket, they are often ready-trimmed, so all you need to do is top and tail finely, remove the outer layer to reveal the smoother stalk underneath, then finely slice it to release all the intoxicating scent. I then rock my knife over the slices, or you could use a mezzaluna or food processor to create very fine flakes. However, the scent and moisture can evaporate very quickly, leaving it dry like sawdust chips. So either cut the stalk only at the very moment you need it, or freeze the slices or flakes immediately, and use them straight from frozen.

The word 'apple' used to be a generic term for any kind of fruit, even nuts. I feel it is not so odd to pair the lemongrass with the apple and mint stuffing, given that the apple originated in Asia, where its wild ancestors still thrive today.

Preheat the oven to 190°C/Fan 170°C/Gas 5 and put a baking tray in there to heat up.

Heat 1 teaspoon of olive oil in a pan over a gentle heat and sweat the onion and garlic with the white wine vinegar for a few minutes till soft. Add the apple and cook for about 5 minutes, then switch off the heat. Stir in the butter to melt into the mixture, then add the mint and parsley, and season with salt and pepper. Set aside for a moment to cool.

Stuff each sea bass with the mixture, tying with string to secure. Brush all over with olive oil, place on the preheated baking tray, which has also been brushed with a little oil, season with salt and pepper and cook for 20 minutes, turning over halfway through.

In the meantime, put the potatoes in a pan of cold water, bring to the boil and simmer for about 5–6 minutes until cooked through but not mushy.

Once the fish is cooked, take it off the tray and place on a plate in the oven to keep warm and to rest, and then put the drained potatoes on the baking tray the fish was cooked on, scatter over a liberal amount of semolina, stir to mix with the oily fish juices, drizzle with some more olive oil if needed and then place under a hot grill for 10–12 minutes or until golden and very crisp, turning over and shaking halfway through.

While the potatoes are under the grill, finely chop the lemongrass and mix straight away with the crème fraîche and a little chopped parsley, ready to serve with the fish and potatoes.

You can use the lemongrass crème fraîche to accompany all sorts of dishes. Leave the parsley out and serve it with fruit too.

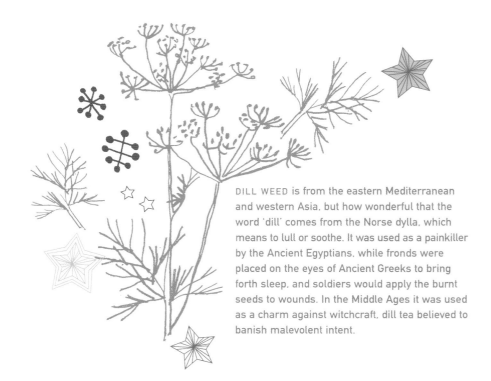

DILL WEED is from the eastern Mediterranean and western Asia, but how wonderful that the word 'dill' comes from the Norse *dylla*, which means to lull or soothe. It was used as a painkiller by the Ancient Egyptians, while fronds were placed on the eyes of Ancient Greeks to bring forth sleep, and soldiers would apply the burnt seeds to wounds. In the Middle Ages it was used as a charm against witchcraft, dill tea believed to banish malevolent intent.

Glass Noodles with Radish, Celery, Cucumber and Dill

SERVES 1 AS A MAIN DISH OR 2 AS A STARTER

1 bundle of rice noodles (about 70g)

75ml soured cream

2 tbsp chopped dill

juice of half a lemon

1 tsp Dijon mustard

2–3 tsp light muscovado sugar, depending upon how sour your lemons are (the dish should have a distinct zing but not be too sour)

2 sticks of celery, thinly sliced

3cm piece of cucumber, quartered and thinly sliced

4 radishes, thinly sliced

I long one day to go whale watching in Scandinavia and marvel beneath the Northern Lights. These cold rice noodles are draped in a sauce made with the cool, clear, glacial flavours of that part of the world. Although it would be very nice on a warm day, I like to eat this when it is pale grey and biting outside, as I find it invigorating. This is probably due to the radish flavours. The French used to serve the Chinese vegetable before a meal, to cleanse the palate.

Remove the paper from the bundle of noodles, place in a bowl or deep plate, cover with boiling water and leave to stand for 5–10 minutes until soft. Rinse in cold water and drain.

Mix the soured cream, dill, lemon juice, mustard and sugar together, then stir in the celery, cucumber and radishes to coat well. Toss with the noodles and eat immediately.

You could try mixing the cream with freshly grated ginger and finely sliced spring onion or mooli instead.

Chestnut, Chorizo and New Potato Tart

What makes this, for me, is the squeeze of lemon over the top at the end, which seems to pull all the flavours together. In particular, it brings the sweet chestnuts in, knitting them together with the potatoes and smoky chorizo. If it is that time of the year, you can use freshly roasted chestnuts. For ease, I buy my chestnuts, probably one of the first foods ever eaten by prehistoric man, in convenient vacuum packs. Late bloomers, the trees do not produce fruit until they are about 40 years old.

Flour your worktop surface and dust flour on the pastry itself. Roll the pastry lightly to about 3mm thick. Gently drape over the rolling pin, then use to line a greased 25cm fluted flan tin (with removable base). Don't stretch the pastry but gently press it into the base and sides. Use a sharp knife to trim the edges. Prick the base with a fork in several places and chill in the fridge for 20 minutes.

Preheat the oven to 200°C/Fan 180°C/Gas 6.

Line your pastry case with baking paper and baking beans and bake blind for 10 minutes. Remove the paper and beans. Take 1 tablespoon of the beaten egg and mix with the milk to create an egg wash, brush all over the pastry and bake for another 10 minutes.

Reduce the oven heat to 180°C/Fan 160°C/Gas 4.

Put the potatoes, chestnuts and chorizo into the pastry case. Beat the cream with the harissa and parsley, then stir in the eggs and season well with salt and pepper. Pour the mixture evenly into the case, over the other ingredients. Scatter with a generous handful of Parmesan and bake for about 30 minutes. Leave to rest for 10 minutes, then squeeze some lemon over the top and serve, perhaps with wilted spinach.

You can, of course, make your own pastry, perhaps wholemeal. Add more harissa if you like it spicier, or maybe even make a chestnut and potato tart with chopped jalapeños and some sliced onions.

SERVES 4–6

plain flour, for dusting

375g ready-rolled shortcrust pastry

3 eggs, beaten

1 tbsp milk

215g very small new potatoes, boiled in skins, cooled and quartered

150g precooked chestnuts, quartered (I use Merchant Gourmet pre-roasted and vacuum-packed ones)

150g ready-to-eat chorizo sausages (the thick ones), skinned, quartered length-ways and cut into pieces about 1cm thick

225ml double cream

1 tbsp harissa paste

a handful of chopped parsley

freshly grated Parmesan

1 lemon

Spaghetti with Edamame and Pecorino

SERVES 1

50–100g spaghetti – cook in
    boiling water for 12 minutes
    or as per packet instructions
2 tbsp mild olive oil
1 garlic clove, crushed
100g shelled edamame, cooked
    (180g in shells)
a few shavings of pecorino

In my local Japanese store they sell pots of ready-cooked edamame, so all I have to do is pop them out of their pods. They have a lovely cleanness and crunch that sits well with the curls of pecorino, salty and fresh like the crests of waves. I make this when I need something very quickly but still want lots of flavour.

Heat the oil in a frying pan and fry the garlic for a few seconds on a low heat until lightly golden. Toss with the spaghetti and edamame, then top with shaved pecorino

Try using wild garlic if you can get it, or make this with broad beans or butter beans instead of the edamame, and maybe with small pieces of feta or toasted halloumi in place of the pecorino.

I SOMETIMES THINK there is no better example of the cross-pollination of food than the noodle-pasta story. Although it is still hotly contested who invented the food, the odds are much in China's favour, with the discovery of a 4,000-year-old bowl of noodles in north-eastern China, amazingly preserved by the Yellow River.

Keema, Chilli and Coriander Pie

My ultimate comfort food, this spiced sort-of-shepherd's-pie has been knocking around for years in Anglo-Indian and British Asian households, often using leftover Indian lamb keema as a base.

My version is loosely based on the first shepherd's pie recipe I ever followed, one of the legendary Delia's. I could have put all the flavourings and spices into the lamb mince, leaving the potato plain, but I decided instead to split them between both layers. If you are not keen on pimping up your potato, you don't have to. You can omit the mushroom and onion altogether and just add some coriander and chilli to the mince instead.

A very important ingredient in this, for me, is the Worcestershire sauce, symbol and legacy of the complex relationship between Britain and India.

This is what I make when the outdoors, and life generally, is inhospitable and harsh, drained of colour. I offer it to friends and family, to nourish them well.

SERVES 6

1 tbsp olive oil, plus extra for brushing
1 large onion, chopped
1 garlic clove, chopped
500g minced lamb
2 tsp garam masala
1/2 tsp ground cinnamon
1 tsp grated fresh ginger (about a 2cm piece of fresh ginger; make sure to squeeze the juice out of the fibres left on the grater)
1 tbsp Worcestershire sauce
1 tbsp plain flour
275ml lamb stock
1 tbsp tomato purée
2 garlic cloves, still in skins

4 baking potatoes, scrubbed
1 tbsp butter
1/2 tsp dried red chilli flakes
juice of half a lemon
1/2 tsp salt
2 chestnut mushrooms, finely chopped
quarter of a red onion, finely chopped
a handful of fresh coriander, finely chopped, stalks included
250g small tomatoes, halved lengthways (I like pomodorino, baby plum tomatoes, but cherry tomatoes would be good too)
a few handfuls of breadcrumbs
grated Parmesan or Cheddar

Heat the oil in a large, deep frying pan. Add the onion and fry on a high heat for 3 minutes to get it nice and browned. Turn the heat down, add the garlic and fry for another minute. Add the mince, turn the heat back up a bit and brown it all over, breaking up any large chunks with a wooden spoon.

Once the mince is browned, turn the heat down again, season with salt and pepper and add 1½ teaspoons of the garam masala, the cinnamon, ginger, Worcestershire sauce and flour, stirring well. Then slowly add the stock, then the tomato purée. Give it all a good stir again, then turn the heat to very low, cover and cook gently for 30 minutes.

Set the oven temperature to 200°C/Fan 180°C/Gas 6. Brush the garlic cloves with a little olive oil, place on a baking tray and put in the oven while it is heating up, until soft in the middle: cooking for about 15–20 minutes.

Meanwhile, place the potatoes whole in their skins in a large pan of cold water and boil for about 20 minutes until soft, then set aside to cool. This method keeps the flesh quite dry and firm inside. When cool, remove the skins with a sharp knife and mash the potato with the soft innards of the garlic cloves, the butter, chilli flakes, remaining ½ teaspoon of garam masala, lemon juice, salt, mushrooms, red onion and coriander. (I tend to run a sharp knife through the potato first so as not to make it too smooth, then add the other ingredients and mix with a fork.)

Place the cooked mince in a casserole or baking dish, add the tomatoes, top with the potato mixture (I don't smooth mine; I like to keep it quite roughed up and rustic-looking). Scatter the breadcrumbs all over, then sprinkle with cheese. Bake in the preheated oven for 25–30 minutes until golden.

You don't have to use Indian keema flavourings. You could spice the lamb any way you like, or even keep the lamb base quite plain and add flavouring to the potato. Why not try a sweet potato mash, or half sweet and half regular potato?

Baked Aubergine Crumbles with Sichuan Pepper

SERVES 4

3 large aubergines
olive oil
1/2 tsp Sichuan pepper
2 garlic cloves, crushed
juice of half a lime
butter, for greasing
50g dried breadcrumbs
50g plump whole rolled oats
2 tbsp grated Cheddar

I like to serve this dish as a starter on a gilt-edged autumn evening. It is made with teardrop aubergines, collapsed in the oven. The aubergine belongs to the gothic-sounding deadly nightshade family, along with its siblings the potato, tomato and capsicum, and indeed this alien fruit from the East initially struck terror in the hearts of people in the West, who thought it was a poison.

I have combined the smoky flesh with a little Sichuan pepper, known in Chinese as 'flower pepper', which is not related to chilli pepper or black pepper. This unusual spice, a component of Chinese five-spice, has a lemony taste and an intriguing numbing heat upon the tongue that I find both bewildering and delicious.

Preheat the oven to 220°C/Fan 200°C/Gas 7.

Brush the aubergines with olive oil, stab in several places, place on a baking tray and bake for 1 hour, turning over once halfway through. When cooked, turn the oven down to 190°C/Fan 170°C/Gas 5. Allow to cool a little first and then cut in half lengthways and scoop out the flesh. Chop up a little with a knife and briefly mash.

Heat 1 tablespoon of olive oil in a pan, add the Sichuan pepper and garlic and fry for a minute. Add the aubergine flesh and lime juice and season with salt, heating the aubergine through for a couple of minutes, stirring from time to time.

Grease the insides of 4 ramekin dishes with a little bit of butter. Divide the aubergine between them.

Place the breadcrumbs in a bowl with the oats, add 3 tablespoons of olive oil and the Cheddar, and mix well. Divide between the ramekins to top the aubergine. Place on a baking tray and bake for 20–25 minutes until golden.

You could, of course, make one large crumble. Try with other vegetables, such as lightly mashed sweet potato or squash, or a bed of chopped stewed tomatoes or mushrooms. The crumble topping is pretty dry, so you could combine with a little cream cheese, quark, goat's cheese or crème fraîche, placing a layer on top of the vegetables and underneath the oaty mixture. Or bash up some leftover nuts and use these in the crumble too, instead of the oats.

Garlic, Herb and Coriander Seed Turkey in Potatoes

SERVES 4

4 baking potatoes, scrubbed

1 tbsp olive oil, plus extra for drizzling

1 onion, thinly sliced

1 garlic clove, crushed

1 tbsp coriander seeds, cracked with a pestle in a mortar

500g turkey mince

3 tbsp white wine

150g Boursin garlic and herb soft cheese

1 tbsp chopped chives, plus extra for garnish

grated Parmesan, for dusting

salad leaves dressed with olive oil and lemon, to serve

This is the kind of thing I would make on returning home from school on autumnal evenings. The coriander seed adds much-needed contrast in texture to an otherwise soft and creamy dish you can eat with just a fork. It is good in-front-of-the-TV food when the winds are ferociously whipping round your four walls outside. It doesn't take too long to make either, especially if you are making a portion for one and using the microwave to cook the potato.

Microwave the potatoes: in my 1,000-watt oven, this takes 30 minutes on the highest setting. In a hot oven – about 220°C/Fan 200°C/Gas 7 – cook for around 1 1/2 hours.

Meanwhile, heat the oil in a pan and fry the onion and garlic on a low heat for about 4 minutes until softened. Add the coriander seeds and fry for a further 5 minutes, stirring occasionally. Add the mince, turn the heat up a bit and fry for 5 minutes, breaking up any lumps with a fork or wooden spoon. Pour in the wine, season with pepper, turn the heat down low, cover and cook for 15 minutes.

Switch off the heat and stir in the Boursin, letting it melt in. Add the chives and set aside.

Preheat the grill to hot. When the potatoes are ready, slice the tops off, carefully scoop out the flesh and place it in a separate bowl. Divide the turkey mixture between the four potato shells. Mash up the leftover potato and top the shells with a mound of mash, using a fork. You won't be able to use all the mashed potato to make the sealed topping, so put the remainder in the fridge or freezer to use in another recipe.

Place the filled potatoes on an oiled baking tray, brush the jackets with olive oil, top with more chopped chives, dust with grated Parmesan and drizzle a little more olive oil over the top. Put under the hot grill for about 10 minutes or until golden and crisp on top. Serve with the salad leaves.

Try with chopped wild mushrooms or leeks instead of mince.

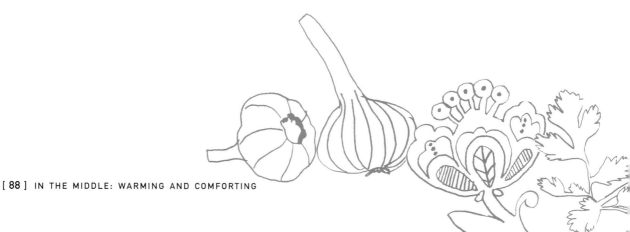

Chicory and Wasabi Bake

This bake was inspired by one from the fabulous Skye Gingell of Petersham Nurseries in Richmond, one of my favourite places. I wanted to make mine with a slightly salty sauce with a touch of bite to lie silkily over the chicory, a hint of bitterness to their clear crunch. The key ingredients here are the anchovy sauce and wasabi. You could use horseradish; I just didn't have any, instead finding wasabi in my fridge left over from sushi.

The anchovy sauce not only adds the saltiness I love but also the umami depth to this dish, making it substantial and heart-warming. It is not that odd a pairing with the wasabi, given that anchovy sauce is based on the fish sauces of the East and chicory has a similar flavour to Chinese leaf. This dish is great with roast beef but it's also lovely on its own with some brown bread, especially when the rain is scratching its way down your windows.

Preheat the oven to 190°C/Fan 170°C/Gas 5.

Trim the ends of the chicory and discard any discoloured outer leaves. Quarter lengthways and arrange cut-side down in an ovenproof dish.

Heat the crème fraîche in a pan, stirring until the consistency has loosened to that of double cream. Switch off the heat and add the anchovy sauce and wasabi paste. Pour this mixture all over the chicory.

Melt the butter and mix with the breadcrumbs. Scatter this all over the chicory and finish with a generous sprinkling of grated Parmesan. Bake for 25 minutes or until golden.

Reduce the anchovy sauce a little and you could do a very nice version with portabella mushrooms, or leeks, or slices of potato and onions.

SERVES 6

6 heads of chicory
500ml crème fraîche
2 tbsp anchovy sauce
2 tsp wasabi paste
50g butter
75g breadcrumbs
freshly grated Parmesan

Chilli Caramel Salmon Pie

Inspired by a mouth-watering Vietnamese salmon dish, I became intrigued by the idea of using a sweet, caramel-based sauce with sour lime and fish sauce. However, I also liked the idea of doing something very comforting with this, like a pie with flaky pastry, some of it remaining golden, crisp and aloof on the side of the plate, some being pushed into the sauce, yielding to it. This dish brings all the assertive vibrancy of Asian road-side flavours into a dull day and on to the little mountain of mashed potato I like to serve alongside.

First make the caramel. The recipe is on page 20.
Preheat the oven to 220°C/Fan 200°C/Gas 7.

Lightly brush a wide oven dish, about 1 litre in capacity, with some groundnut oil, including the edges where the pastry will sit. Put the salmon and red pepper in the dish.

Heat the 2 tablespoons of groundnut oil in a pan, add the shallots and toss for 4–5 minutes over a medium to high heat until golden. Turn the heat down to quite low and add the garlic and some black pepper and fry for another minute. Switch the heat off and stir in the peanut butter. It will start to melt and gradually be easier to stir into the shallots. Pour this over the salmon and red pepper in the dish. Sprinkle the chillies and ginger over the top.

Gently heat the caramel over a low heat, stirring to loosen and soften, then stir in the fish sauce and lime juice, stirring well, and then finally the flour. Pour over the rest of the ingredients in the dish. Scatter the coriander and spring onions over the top. Carefully stir to mix it all a bit.

Place the pastry over the top of the dish to seal. I roll mine out a little first, just enough to loosen it up a bit and make sure it will fit. Lay over the dish and trim the edges with a sharp knife and crimp with a fork to seal it right down. Brush with beaten egg and bake for 25–30 minutes until golden. Rest for 10 minutes before serving.

You could make this with chicken pieces. You might also like to make individual pot pies.

SERVES 6

caramel (see page 20)
2 tbsp groundnut oil, plus extra for oiling the dish
800g salmon fillets (about 5), each fillet skinned and cut into 4
1 red pepper, sliced
200g shallots (about 15), halved lengthways
2 garlic cloves, sliced
6 tbsp no-added-sugar crunchy peanut butter
2 large red chillies, deseeded and thinly sliced
a piece of fresh ginger, about 4cm x 2cm, peeled and cut into thin sticks
3 tbsp fish sauce
juice of 2 limes: about 3 tbsp
1 tbsp plain flour
a handful of fresh coriander, chopped, stalks included
6 spring onions, sliced chunkily on the diagonal
375g ready-rolled puff pastry
1 egg, beaten

Crumbled Lincolnshire Sausage, Cranberry, Olive and Lemon Pasta

SERVES 2

olive oil

4 Lincolnshire sausages

4 rashers of streaky bacon, finely diced, or some finely diced pancetta

half a red onion, sliced

a few slices of lemon

1 tsp crushed chillies in oil or some finely chopped fresh red or green chilli

enough pasta for 2 people

a handful of cranberries, finely sliced

a handful of black olives

a handful of baby spinach, shredded

crème fraîche, for binding

Christmas is the biggest culinary event of my calendar. Although my family is not Christian, for some reason we have always taken Christmas very seriously. My mother recalls fond memories of school church visits, carols and hymns, and she honours the Virgin Mary – a couple of beautiful, tiny idols collected from travels abroad watch over our home.

Another example of cooking for practical necessity, this dish was first created to use up some post-Christmas ingredients in a lighter dish: some crumbled sausage meat, bacon, fresh cranberries and spinach. However, my mother liked the taste so much she requested I make it over and over again, loving the nuggets of crispy meat and the ruby flickers of cranberry sourness.

Preheat the oven to 200°C/Fan 180°C/Gas 6.

Heat a baking tray drizzled with a bit of olive oil. Cut off the end of each sausage and squeeze the meat out of the skins, crumbling into small amounts on to the baking sheet. Add the bacon, onion, lemon and chilli to the pan, drizzle over a bit more olive oil, and roast the whole lot for about 25 minutes or until the bacon and sausagemeat are crispy.

Boil the pasta in water for 12 minutes or as per packet instructions and then toss with everything from the baking tray, plus the cranberries, olives and spinach, with a few spoonfuls of crème fraîche to bind it all together.

I used Lincolnshire sausages because we had them, but you can squeeze out the insides of any sausages, including chipolatas. And, by all means, swap the black olives for green.

Baked Sausages with Tomato, Balsamic and Cumin

A deeply aromatic spice, from Egypt and Syria, my beloved cumin is the seed of a plant with tiny white flowers, blooming in small umbrella-shaped clusters.

The nuttiness of the cumin works really well in this hearty dish, which is as cosy as a faithful cardigan with little bobbles and stretched cuffs. Cumin balances the oozing tomatoes and sticky balsamic, tarring onto the crisp skin of the sausages.

Preheat the oven to 200°C/Fan 180°C/Gas 6.

Put 2 or 3 sausages for each person on a baking dish, place in the oven and cook for about 25 minutes.

In the meantime, boil the potatoes in their skins for about 5 minutes or until soft, then drain. With skins still on, crush the potatoes with a fork. Add the crème fraîche, the spring onions and some freshly ground black pepper, and stir in.

About seven minutes before the end of the cooking time for the sausages, add the cumin seeds to the baking dish and stir into the hot fat. Allow to sizzle in the oven for a minute or so before adding the balsamic vinegar, cherry tomatoes and basil leaves – all straight into the pan and swished around with the juices. You could add some dried red chilli, too.

Serve the sausages and the sauce over a bed of the creamy potatoes.

You could use another spice instead of cumin, such as coriander seeds, freshly cracked pepper or maybe even some wholegrain mustard. You might like to add a splash of red wine vinegar, maybe with some red wine itself, instead of the balsamic vinegar.

SERVES 2

4–6 sausages of your choice
12 small or salad potatoes, scrubbed
1 tbsp crème fraîche
2 spring onions, chopped
2 tsp cumin seeds
2 tablespoons balsamic vinegar, preferably the thick glaze kind
a handful of cherry tomatoes
a handful of basil leaves
dried red chilli flakes (optional)

Baked Haddock with Spiced Breadcrumbs and Gobi

This dish has quite a lot of spices, which are brought to life by the acidity of the yoghurt added to the breadcrumb mix. The yoghurt works well with the baked haddock flesh, too, so I complement the dish by serving another small, cool, spoonful of yoghurt alongside.

SERVES 2

2 tsp olive oil, plus extra for brushing
1 small onion, finely chopped
1 garlic clove, finely chopped
1 plum tomato, chopped
½ small green finger chilli, finely chopped
1 tsp grated fresh ginger
½ tsp salt or a few good pinches
½ tsp garam masala
couple of pinches of turmeric
splash of lemon juice
a handful of chopped coriander
½ small cauliflower, about 270g, florets and small leaves chopped up

2 large or 4 small haddock fillets
half a lemon
ground cumin (optional)
natural yoghurt and chopped cucumber, to serve

FOR THE BREADCRUMBS

100g day-old bread (sourdough is nice for this)
1 tbsp olive oil
3 generous pinches of each of the following: ground cumin, ground cinnamon, ground coriander, salt
2 tbsp butter, melted
2 tbsp natural yoghurt

Heat the oil in a pan, add the onion and gently fry for 3 minutes, then add the garlic and fry for about another minute and a half or until lightly golden. Add the tomato, chilli, ginger, salt, garam masala, turmeric, lemon juice and coriander and stir well. Add 2 tablespoons of water and fry gently for a few minutes until the mixture is quite shiny. Add the cauliflower, stir well to coat, add another 4 tablespoons of water, stir again, cover and steam through on a low heat for 10 minutes or until the cauliflower is soft.

Preheat the oven to 180°C/Fan 160°C/Gas 4.

Tear the bread into small pieces, place on a preheated tray and bake for about 8 minutes until dry and crisp. Turn the oven up to 190°C/Fan 170°C/Gas 5. Whizz the bread to breadcrumbs in a food processor.

Heat the olive oil in a pan, add the breadcrumbs, the cumin, cinnamon, coriander and salt, and a grind of black pepper. Fry for about 3–5 minutes or until golden, then drain on kitchen paper. In a bowl, combine the breadcrumbs with the butter and yoghurt.

Brush a baking tray with olive oil, put the fillets on it and press the breadcrumb mixture on top of the fish to create a crust. Squeeze over some lemon and add a final pinch of ground cumin, if you wish. Bake for about 25 minutes.

Serve with natural yoghurt and some chopped cucumber.

Instead of gobi, you could substitute small pieces of potato. You can use the breadcrumbs with any fish, and also to coat chicken or to top gratins.

Plum and Coriander Ribs

SERVES 2–4

about 850g pork ribs

1 tbsp grated fresh ginger

2 garlic cloves, crushed

5 tbsp plum sauce

1 tsp ketchup

1 tsp dried red chilli flakes

2 tbsp coriander seeds, cracked
    with a pestle in a mortar

2 tsp ground coriander

1 tbsp maple syrup

1 tsp dark brown sugar

2 tbsp olive oil

fresh coriander, to serve

This really could not be simpler – you just mix everything together and pour it into a roasting tin. So easy and yet so well received. The ribs are sticky, moreish and the perfect food to gnaw. I served this to some friends, one of whom was heartbroken, and the dish seemed to cheer her up substantially.

Mix everything together with the ribs, rubbing the mixture into them, then cover and leave out to marinate for 1 hour minimum, or refrigerate for longer. Overnight is best.

Preheat the oven to 180°C/Fan 160°C/Gas 4.

Pour the ribs and marinade into a large roasting tin and cook for 1 hour until brown and crispy, turning over halfway. Serve scattered with fresh coriander.

Use this mixture to marinate chicken thighs for a barbecue, or even fillets of salmon. You could tear up the meat and eat it hot in wraps or baguettes, too.

Lapsang Souchong-scented Salmon with Nutmeg Butter and Kale

Centuries ago, the Chinese began to add tea leaves to the fire that was used to smoke fish and duck. Originally this process was used to help to preserve the food, but later became a way of adding depth of flavour. Wanting to impart the fragrance of tea but without enduring the billowing smoke that fills the kitchen when tea-smoking fish with foil in a wok, I thought I'd use this technique for a subtler version, which I call tea-steaming. I thought it would be easier, and less messy, to simply use a tea bag rather than loose leaves in the pouch with the water, allowing the scent to delicately infuse the tender flesh.

The smoky-bacon scent of the lapsang souchong laces the fish as it steams. I serve it with ribbons of kale for a delicately pefumed but warming meal.

SERVES 2
whole nutmeg
25g butter, softened
oil, for greasing
2 salmon fillets
2 lapsang souchong tea bags
shredded kale for 2 people

Preheat the oven to 200°C/Fan 180°C/Gas 6.

Grate some nutmeg into the butter, then shape into a log, wrap in cling film and refrigerate until cold and solid.

Line a roasting tin with 2 sheets of foil, big enough to fold over and wrap the salmon fillets in. I do it so the lining is three times the length of the tin, with plenty on either side to fold over and tuck in. Oil an area big enough for the salmon fillets, then place the salmon there with the tea bags next to them, and pour 3 tablespoons of boiling water over each tea bag. Fold over the foil to create a pouch, ensuring that the fillets and tea bags sit in a single layer and do not touch each other. Cook for 15 minutes.

Put the kale in a frying pan with a sprinkle of water and stir-fry until cooked through but still crunchy, and serve with a little of the nutmeg butter on top of it, alongside the tea-scented salmon.

You can use any type of tea bag you like to scent fish in this way – from Earl Grey to the entrancingly named Moonlit Jasmine.

Rioja Chicken with Polenta Cakes

SERVES 4–6

2 tbsp olive oil, plus extra for
brushing

1 large onion, chopped

8 garlic cloves, finely sliced

60g chorizo sausage, not the
slices, but the sausage,
skinned and diced

1 chicken stock cube

250ml Rioja (Spanish red wine)

400g can of chopped tomatoes

1 tsp dark muscovado sugar

1 bay leaf

1 large chicken, about 2kg

500g ready-cooked polenta

zest of 1 lemon

1 tbsp lemon juice

¼ tsp crushed chillies in oil

a good handful of fresh
coriander leaves, chopped

crème fraîche, soured cream or
thick yoghurt, to serve

It is such a rewarding feeling when you create a dish that you are so happy with you feel it could be one of the best things you have ever cooked. I felt that way about this meal. Everything about it, from the almost obscene juiciness of the meat, to the robustly flavoured sauce and the sizzling golden polenta cakes, just worked so well. I had only used polenta cut into slabs before, so had no real idea what it was going to turn out like, whizzing it up into crumbs and then reshaping it with chilli and coriander, but it worked a treat. I love how, unlike most Indian dishes, which are cooked on the hob and need frequent attention, you just put everything for this in a pot and it bubbles in the oven, emerging transformed and beautiful, as though a fairy godmother of food has waved her magic wand over the ingredients and bequeathed you a feast.

Preheat the oven to 180°C/Fan 160°C/Gas 4.

Heat the oil in a pan, add the onion and garlic and cook for about 5 minutes until softened and slightly browned. Add the chorizo and cook for about another 4 minutes before crumbling in the stock cube and stirring to mix.

Transfer this mixture into a 2.5-litre casserole pot with a lid, in which the chicken can sit comfortably. Stir the wine, tomatoes, sugar and bay leaf into the onion mixture. Place the chicken on top and cook, covered, with the lid for 1 hour.

Take off the lid, brush the chicken with olive oil and season it. Return it to the oven and cook, uncovered, for another hour, or until golden.

During the last half an hour of the chicken's cooking time, cut the polenta up into small pieces, then, using your hands, squeeze these pieces to break up and crumble them. Place it in a food processor and whizz till it looks like lumpy breadcrumbs. Add the lemon zest and juice, chillies and coriander and pulse a couple of times until well mixed with the polenta.

Preheat the grill to hot. Press and shape the processed mixture into small patties. Place them on a baking tray, brush with oil and put under the hot grill for about 6 minutes until golden. The patties will have become very soft on the underside so turn them over very carefully using a fish slice or palette knife, so as not to break, then grill the other side for about 6 minutes to become golden and crisp.

When the chicken's hour is up, carefully lift it out from the pot, draining all juices from inside the chicken back into the pot, and place on a board to rest before carving.

Ladle all the sauce from the pot into a pan and bring to the boil. Continue to cook until reduced by half and you have a rich, thick sauce.

Serve pieces of the chicken with the sauce, polenta cakes and some crème fraîche, soured cream or thick yoghurt.

Try porcini and basil polenta cakes. If you like things hotter, add a few whole dried chillies to the pot of chicken.

Leg of Lamb with Black Cherries, Tamarind and Walnut

SERVES 6–8

olive oil

1 leg of lamb, about 2 kg

peeled cloves of 3 garlic bulbs

250ml lamb stock

1/2 tsp tamarind concentrate

30–40 dark cherries (about 350g), stoned and quartered

1 tbsp walnut oil

100g walnut pieces

There is little I find more sublime than a cherry. I am so in love with them and could happily eat them all day every day if they weren't so horribly expensive.

This recipe is for lamb cooked extremely slowly, wrapped in the manner of Greek kleftiko, on a bed of garlic which is then boiled up with the juices to make a rich gravy. The smidgeon of tamarind I use is from concentrate: about 50 pence a pot, it lasts me an age. Chopped dark cherries and broken walnuts are finally stirred in to create a sauce both complex and comforting.

Preheat the oven to 180°C/Fan 160°C/Gas 4.

Heat 2 tbsp of olive oil on a baking tray on the hob and brown the leg of lamb all over. Line a roasting tin with 2 sheets of foil, and then a sheet of baking parchment on top, big enough to fold over and wrap the lamb in. I do it so the lining is three times the length of the tin, with plenty on either side to fold over and tuck in.

Put the garlic cloves in the tin on top of the baking parchment, place the lamb on top of the garlic, then pour the stock over. Wrap the baking parchment over the lamb, sealing well and tucking the ends in, then fold the foil over and do the same, tucking in around the edges. Cook the lamb for 4 hours.

Open out the foil and paper, cutting away the extra lengths from each side. Brush the lamb with oil, grind over some black pepper and scatter with some sea salt, and cook for another 30 minutes until nice and brown.

Remove the lamb and place on a plate or board to rest. In the meantime, put the garlic cloves and all the juices from the roasting tin into a pan, add 60ml water and the tamarind concentrate and simmer gently for 3 minutes. Switch off the heat and stir in the cherries.

Heat the walnut oil in a frying pan and toast the walnuts for a few minutes until golden, then add them to the cherry sauce.

I serve this with potatoes – mashed, roasted, or creamed and then piped on to a tray and baked until golden and crisp on the outside. You could use balsamic instead of the tamarind, and try plums instead of the cherries. A similar sauce would go with lamb chops

Roasted Onions with Pear Juice, Dijon Mustard and Mozzarella

SERVES 4–6

8 onions, mixed colours if you like

olive oil

sea salt

150ml Peartiser or similar sparkling pear juice or even some regular pear juice

10g butter

2 tsp Dijon mustard

1 ball of mozzarella, or any other cheese for melting, such as Gruyère or fontina

A dish of red and white onion bulbs can look beautiful, a wintry centrepiece exquisite enough to rival a bowl of pouting summer blooms. Although they can be eaten alone, this makes a wonderful side dish for a roast, such as rib of beef.

Preheat the oven to 190°C/Fan 170°C/Gas 5.

Peel the onions and cut a sliver off the base so they can stand up but don't cut through the base. Cut down crossways into each onion to almost quarter, but not right through to the base. Stand in an ovenproof dish and brush with olive oil and rub with a bit of sea salt.

Gently heat the Peartiser in a pan and add a knob of butter and the mustard. Stir briskly, then, when the butter has melted and the mustard dissolved, pour this over the onions, cover with foil and bake for 30 minutes. Then remove the foil, spoon the juices over the onions and bake for another 30 minutes. Cut the cheese into 8 pieces and divide between the onions, pushing a piece into the centre of each. Season with black pepper and bake for another 5 minutes until melted, grilling the top of the cheese if you prefer.

Brie is also excellent for this. Try using perry or cider instead of the pear juice.

THE ANCIENT EGYPTIANS worshipped the onion. To them, its concentric rings represented eternity, and they immortalised the vegetable in gold. Onion traces were found in the burial of Rameses IV, laid in his eye sockets, with the hope that the strong scent would pull him back from the hereafter.

Garam Masala Chicken with Basil Couscous

SERVES 4

3 tbsp oil

2 tsp cumin seeds

4 cloves

1 bay leaf

1 onion, roughly chopped, plus
    half an onion, sliced

2 garlic cloves, roughly chopped

125g canned chopped tomatoes

2 green chillies, finely chopped

1 tsp grated fresh ginger

1 tsp salt

2½ tsp garam masala

1 tsp ground turmeric

a handful of fresh coriander,
    chopped

4 chicken legs

With the turn of a key in my parents' front door, it is easy to regress to being 13 again, comforted by the sight of my father in the kitchen, proudly adding the final touches to his signature chicken dishes, rice steaming away and an abundant bowl of spiced cucumber raita marinating in the fridge, patiently awaiting my return.

Often the next day there would be leftover chicken, the deep garam masala flavours intensifying overnight. Couscous is effortlessly quick and I love this finer grain with the chicken, soaking up all the sauce into its soft mushiness. I used basil leaf one day instead of my usual coriander to add flavour to the couscous, and I loved the flavour of it with the sauce.

Preheat the oven to 200°C/Fan 180°C/Gas 6.

Heat the oil in a pan with the cumin seeds, cloves and bay leaf. When the seeds are sizzling, add the chopped onion and garlic, leaving the sliced onion aside for later. Cover and cook on a low heat for 15 minutes. Switch off the heat, remove the bay leaf and cloves and set aside.

Using a slotted spoon, transfer the onion, garlic and cumin to a blender or grinder and whizz until smooth, leaving the oil in the pan. Put the pan with the oil back on the heat and, when hot, add the blended onion mixture. Fry until golden brown. Remove the pan from the heat for a few seconds and add the tomatoes, chillies, ginger, salt, garam masala, turmeric and chopped coriander. Add a splash of water and cook on a low heat, stirring.

When the mixture is shiny and the oil has begun to separate a little, switch off the heat and stir in 250ml water.

Place the chicken legs and onion slices in an ovenproof dish, pour the sauce over the top and cook in the oven for 30 minutes, or until the chicken is cooked and the sauce bubbling.

When the chicken is nearly ready, prepare the couscous. Place the grains in a large bowl with 400ml boiling water and the butter. Stir, cover and leave to stand for 5 minutes. Fluff with a fork to separate and stir in the basil and lime.

Serve the chicken with the couscous.

FOR THE BASIL COUSCOUS
250g couscous
knob of butter
handful of basil leaves, torn
squeeze of lime juice

ONE CHRISTIAN MYTH holds that as Satan left the Garden of Eden, garlic sprung from his left footprint. So unlike the Roman legionnaires, who believed it gave them courage, strength and stamina. Even the workers who built the great pyramids of Giza went on a rare strike when their promised supply ran out. And we all know of garlic's supposed powers to ward off vampires, mosquitoes, snakes and general all-round evilness. Given that it has antibacterial and antiparasitic qualities, it might indeed keep away delusional fevers.

Beef Stewed with Miso, Barley and Sun-kissed Tomatoes

SERVES 6

olive oil

1½ kg boneless cubed beef

2 onions, sliced

1 garlic clove, finely chopped

400g can of chopped tomatoes

550ml beef stock

3 tbsp organic brown rice miso paste

150g pearl barley, thoroughly washed

140g sun-kissed tomatoes (I buy these in a 280g jar preserved in olive oil)

fresh parsley, chopped, to garnish

I decided to use some of miso's intense salty flavour to add depth to a beef stew, with texture added by barley, and colour and vivacity bestowed by shiny, scarlet sun-kissed tomatoes. The barley makes the meal complete, creating a dish that will fortify you.

Preheat the oven to 170°C/Fan 150°C/Gas 3.

Heat 1 tablespoon of olive oil in a large frying pan. Brown the beef, in about 4 batches, over a medium heat. Place the browned meat in a 2.5-litre casserole dish.

Add the onion to the frying pan and fry until golden brown on a medium heat. Turn the heat down and add the garlic, frying for another minute to soften. Transfer to the meat in the casserole dish, add the canned tomatoes, beef stock and miso, and stir well.

Cover and cook in the centre of the oven for 2 hours, stirring every half an hour and adding extra water if it gets too dry. It needs to have a decent amount of sauce.

Add the barley with 120ml water and cook for another hour. Add the sun-kissed tomatoes for the last 20 minutes, stirring well. Garnish with a scattering of parsley.

Try using lamb instead of beef, or halved baby plum tomatoes instead of sun-kissed or sun-dried tomatoes.

ALTHOUGH MISO has only begun to enjoy mainstream popularity in the West over the past few years, it goes all the way back to fourth-century China. Miso is made from soy beans that have been fermented with salt, a mould culture and a grain, usually rice or barley. It is then aged: the darker it is, the stronger the flavour. Thus you can get miso ranging from virginal white to dark brown, which has a rich, mature umami flavour. Buddhist monks were responsible for bringing it to Japan around the 17th century, refining and incorporating it into the diet of legendary Samurai warriors. It later became a staple for all Japanese, with different varieties emerging in the various provinces. In mythology, miso is believed to be a gift from the heavens, bringing happiness, good health and long life. It wouldn't surprise me if there were some truth in this.

Confit of Duck Leg with Pine Nut Couscous and Date Chutney

You might imagine that confit of duck leg must be terribly complicated. It is true that it has to sit around in salt for an entire day, but that's all it does. Sit. First in salt, then in fat, then by itself, while the skin crisps to the stuff of my dreams. It isn't a difficult process and is very worth the wait. The way the flesh is cooked, ultra tender, reminds me of Middle Eastern meats, and so I like it paired with fluffy couscous and sweet dates sharpened up with a little vinegar.

Place the duck legs in a casserole dish large enough to contain them side by side, and their fat, and rub well with the salt, pepper and juniper mixture. Cover with cling film and marinate in the fridge for 24 hours, turning over once after 12 hours.

Rinse the marinade off the duck legs thoroughly and pat dry very well. Preheat the oven to 160°C/Fan 140°C/Gas 3.

Return the duck legs to the casserole and pour over the fat, making sure the legs are completely submerged. Cover with foil, pierce a few times and cook in the centre of the oven for 3 hours. Leave to cool in the fat and then, when at room temperature, chill in the fridge if not using straight away.

When ready to use the duck legs, preheat the oven to 200°C/Fan 180°C/Gas 6. Take the legs out of the fat, wiping excess fat away, and place skin-side up on a roasting tray. Roast for 40 minutes until crisp.

While roasting, make the date chutney. Heat the oil, add the onion and garlic and allow to sweat through on a low heat for about 3–4 minutes. Set aside to cool a little, then place in a food processor with the ready-to-eat dates.

Place the chunks of dried dates in a bowl, pour 200ml boiling water over them and leave to soak for 15 minutes. Pour this into the food processor with the onion mixture, add the chillies, lime juice and white wine vinegar, and pulse to a chutney consistency. Not completely smooth or a paste but with very small pieces of onion and date still discernable. Season with salt and pepper.

Place the couscous in a large bowl with 400ml boiling water and the butter. Stir, cover and leave to stand for 5 minutes. Fluff with a fork to separate the grains.

Toast the pine nuts in a dry non-stick pan. Add to the couscous with the fresh mint and a squeeze of lime.

Serve the confit with simple greens, roasted carrots or potato instead of the couscous.

SERVES 4

FOR THE CONFIT

4 duck legs
4 tbsp rock salt
2 tsp crushed black pepper
3 crushed juniper berries
    (I place the salt and pepper in a mortar, put the berries on top and use a pestle to press down and crush the berries into the salt and pepper)
500g duck fat (or use goose fat or enough vegetable oil to completely submerge the duck if you can't get hold of duck fat)

FOR THE CHUTNEY AND COUSCOUS

1 tsp olive oil
1 onion, chopped
1 garlic clove, chopped
6 ready-to-eat dates, chopped
100g of a block of dried, stone-out, dates, cut into chunks
1/2 tsp crushed chillies in oil
1 tbsp lime juice
1 tbsp white wine vinegar
250g couscous
a knob of butter
100g pine nuts
a handful of fresh mint leaves, chopped
1 lime

Steamed Hoki with Crushed Coriander and Crispy Onions

SERVES 4

1 green chilli, finely chopped

4 garlic cloves, finely chopped

2 large handfuls of chopped
   fresh coriander

1 tsp whole coriander seeds

½ tsp salt

½ tsp garam masala

3 tbsp oil (I use sunflower or
   mild olive)

1 onion, finely sliced

4 thick hoki fillets, or any other
   firm white fish you prefer

1 lime, quartered

1 onion, very finely sliced and
   crisply fried in oil, to serve

On dark and thunderous days I like to defy the slate sky with the brightest of coriander. Like a medieval diner, I scatter this herb as though it were pepper. This recipe indulges my coriander habit, the main flavouring for parcels of snowy-white hoki fillets. Even if the rooftops and cobbles outside are being thoroughly drenched, the emerald hue of this leaf brings a brightness to the plate.

Preheat the oven to 180°C/Fan 160°C/Gas 4.

Place the chilli, garlic, coriander leaves and seeds, salt and garam masala in a blender and whizz to a paste, or pound with a pestle in a mortar. Heat the oil in a pan and add the sliced onion, cook for a few minutes until soft and light golden. Add the paste and gently heat through.

Place the hoki fillets on a piece on foil. Spoon the paste over the top, wrap the foil to create a pouch and cook in the oven for 12–15 minutes or until cooked through.

Serve with lime wedges and the crisp onions.

Try making this with basil instead, or add some grated coconut to the coriander paste for a Keralan taste. You could even add a few Thai dried shrimp for a richer flavour.

Baked Monkfish with Harissa and Parma Ham

Harissa, the North African dense chilli paste, is such a versatile and useful ingredient, and full of the flavours that switch me on. I use the rose harissa from Belazu, now found in many supermarkets, frequently adding a little to stews, soups and dips, rubbing it into meat or stirring into the simmering water for rice. Here, I use it to wipe meaty monkfish before wrapping up in Parma ham, adding a quick squeeze of lemon before doing so to wake all the flavours up.

Preheat the oven to 190°C/Fan 170°C/Gas 5 and heat up a baking tray. Cut each fillet in half widthways. Smear each fillet with a little harissa paste, rubbing it in a bit. Squeeze over a little lemon juice and then wrap each fillet in a piece of Parma ham, tucking the ends underneath. Place on a lightly oiled hot baking tray. Drizzle with olive oil and bake for 12–15 minutes. Serve with some of the oily, harissa-flavoured juices poured over the top.

Try smearing a little pesto or sun-dried tomato paste over the fish before wrapping in ham.

SERVES 4

2 monkfish tail fillets, about
    150g each, skinless, boneless,
    washed and patted dry
harissa paste
4 slices of Parma ham
olive oil
juice of 1 lemon

Foil-baked Feta

SERVES 4

4 x 200g blocks of feta cheese

extra virgin olive oil, a generous
slug for each pouch

2 garlic cloves, very thinly sliced

1 tsp dried red chilli flakes

a handful of oregano leaves,
finely chopped

4 fresh plum tomatoes, chopped

2 tsp tomato purée

a handful of capers

half a red onion, thinly sliced

It had never occurred to me to heat feta until my Greek friends presented me with a blisteringly hot foil packet of the baked cheese on a wind-blasted beach in Mykonos. It still holds its shape, just softening and mellowing, and is delicious mopped up with crusty bread to soak up the green and red juices.

Preheat the oven to 200°C/Fan 180°C/Gas 6.

Create 4 individual foil pouches by tearing off 4 large strips of foil and placing a block of feta on each with enough foil to wrap over. Divide the rest of the ingredients between the feta, fold up the foil and bake for 10 minutes.

Serve with lots of fresh bread.

You could try this simple version, just with olive oil and pepper. Or maybe you would like to use basil or coriander or fresh mint leaves? Or perhaps cut the feta into chunks and tip it all into a large baking dish with chopped tomatoes, a crumbled chicken stock cube, olive oil and herbs for one big serving.

Saffron Quails Stuffed with Ricotta, Garlic and Gooseberry Mash

This is not the thing to make if you are in an impatient mood. You need to be a little bit slow and careful when placing the stuffing under the delicate skin, gently teasing it away from the flesh a bit at a time. Any haste might result in tearing. I buy quails ready-prepared for roasting, so all I have to do is stuff them and place them straight in the oven. You could serve one of these fragile, tiny birds each as a starter or two as a main. If picking away at the minute bones is just too much bother, buy boned quails and stuff those instead.

I had a can of gooseberries leftover from pie-making, but you could use a few fresh ones, chopped and stewed slightly first in a little sugar and white wine, so not too tart. Although not as commonly used today, they reached the heights of popularity in 19th-century Britain, with people even joining gooseberry clubs. I foresee a revival.

SERVES 2–4
4 garlic cloves, unpeeled
olive oil, for brushing
1 large potato, scrubbed
3 tbsp ricotta cheese
300g can of gooseberries in juice, drained
a pinch of saffron strands
4 prepared quails, ready for roasting

Preheat the oven to 200°C/Fan 180°C/Gas 6.

Brush the garlic skins with oil and, while the oven is heating up, roast in the oven on a tray for about 15–20 minutes until soft. Place the potato whole and still in its skin in a pan and cover with water. Bring to the boil and boil for about 20 minutes till soft. Remove the skin with a sharp knife and mash the flesh, then leave to cool.

Squeeze out the garlic from the skins, chop finely and mix into the mash with the ricotta and season very well. Halve 20 of the gooseberries and gently mix in, taking care not to mash them in too much.

Steep the saffron in a teaspoon of hot water.

Gently pull the skin back on each of the quails and stuff the mixture under the skin/ Be careful not to overstuff or the skin will split while roasting. Place any remainder in the cavities, along with the remaining gooseberries. Brush olive oil over the quail skin and rub in a little saffron liquid all over.

Place in an oiled roasting tin and cook for 35 minutes or until the juices run clear when pierced with a skewer at the thickest part of the thigh.

You can use this stuffing for a chicken or turkey instead. You could also shape into balls and bake or fry to go alongside plainly roasted breast fillets.

Pork with Green Peppercorns, Water Chestnuts and Lemon

SERVES 4

1 tbsp olive oil

4 thick prime pork loin steaks
(about 200g each), seasoned
with salt and pepper

300ml whole milk

pared rind of 1 unwaxed lemon

25g butter

4 garlic cloves, halved
lengthways

1 chicken stock cube

3 tbsp double cream

2 tsp green peppercorns in
brine, drained

12 water chestnuts, sliced

This dish was inspired by a recipe for a whole pork loin baked with milk and orange. Here I gently cook steaks in milk infused with a few curls of lemon rind. I love the refreshing snap of the water chestnuts with the lemony, creamy sauce, a gentle backdrop for the green peppercorns whose heat ignites the palate.

Preheat the oven to 160°C/Fan 140°C/Gas 3.

Heat the oil in a large frying pan and cook the seasoned steaks for a minute or so on each side over a medium heat until golden. Drain on kitchen paper and place in a baking dish where they can sit snugly side by side.

Bring the milk to just under boiling with the lemon rind. Season with a little white pepper.

Melt the butter in another saucepan. Add the garlic and cook for a couple of minutes, then pour over the pork in the dish. Pour the milk and lemon over the pork too. Cover with foil and place in the oven for 30 minutes.

Remove the chops, put the lemon peel aside for now and strain the liquid into a pan. Crumble in the stock cube, bring to the boil and boil for 5 minutes. Stir in the cream, peppercorns, water chestnuts and the lemon peel, and heat through.

Slice the pork and serve with the sauce. This is good with buttered noodles or mashed potato.

You might like to use sliced leeks instead of the water chestnuts, or onions. Or maybe omit the peppercorns and chestnuts and just have the lemon sauce, perhaps served with some spinach. Or for a completely different approach, a lemon and flaked almond sauce instead, crumbling a handful of flaked almonds into the lemon sauce at the end.

Drumsticks with Sesame, Five-Spice and Coca-Cola

MAKES 6 DRUMSTICKS

6 chicken drumsticks, skinned
20 shallots, halved lengthways
groundnut oil, for drizzling
225ml Coca-Cola
1/2 tsp plain flour
2 spring onions, finely sliced

FOR THE MARINADE

2 tsp ground five-spice
3 tsp sesame seeds, plus extra
    for scattering at the end
1/2 tsp ground ginger
4 garlic cloves, crushed
1 tsp dark brown sugar
1 tsp dark soy sauce
a piece of fresh ginger, about
    6cm x 3.5cm, grated
1 tsp groundnut oil

Roasting marinated drumsticks one night for friends, I found they were a little too dry, that they needed some liquid. All I had was a can of cola – so I used that. I liked the sort of Deep American South feel of the cola with the barbecued-style chicken, the five-spice giving it depth and warmth. Although I use it instead of Cajun spice, it evokes old New Orleans, mysterious voodoo-filled neighbourhoods, the smoky intoxicating scent rising above pavements and puffs of tobacco, where old men sit and drink burning shots of whisky.

Combine the marinade ingredients together. Slash the drumsticks a couple of times on the fattest part. Rub in the marinade and chill overnight. At the very least leave for an hour.

Preheat the oven to 200°C/Fan 180°C/Gas 6.

Place the shallots in a deep roasting tin, drizzle some groundnut oil over and shake the pan thoroughly to coat. Place a rack in the tin over the shallots and place the drumsticks on top, patting all the marinade on top of the chicken pieces. Drizzle with a little more groundnut oil and roast in the oven for 15 minutes. Turn the drumsticks over and roast for another 10 minutes. Pour the cola over and roast for another 10 minutes.

Remove the chicken from the rack and set aside, pouring the shallots and all the cola juices into a saucepan. Briskly stir in the flour and bring to the boil, then boil without stirring for a few minutes until reduced by half into a thick sauce. Serve with the chicken and some spring onions and some more sesame seeds.

I sometimes serve this with just plain white rice. Indeed, you might like to add some whisky instead of the cola, increasing the sugar in the marinade and omitting the five-spice. Or you might like to exchange freshly grated orange zest for the five-spice.

Upside-down Spiced Butter Chicken

This is an adaptation of my good friend Marianne Lumb's version of Simon Hopkinson's roast chicken. We first met, and made this, when she came over to teach me how to wield a knife. We never used large knives or chopping boards at home, except for meat. Instead, we would chop vegetables in our hands using small paring knives, straight into the pan. I had done this a couple of times on television and it had to be qualified with a health and safety comment. I thought I had better learn and so super-talented Marianne came to teach me. The trick, I found, to the ultra-fast chef chopping is that it is not 'up and down' but a continuous circular movement. Chatting over a flurry of steel blades, we made this dish, which I thought was a wonderful way to get a succulent, juicy, golden roast chicken. It never fails me.

This recipe is freestyle play time – use whichever flavourings or spices you like. Pull out what you have in your cupboards and see what you might like to add to the butter. Don't measure. I make it different every time, chucking in whatever I am in the mood for.

SERVES 4–6
110g butter, softened
dried spices and fresh herbs
    of choice
1.8kg chicken
1 lemon, halved

Preheat the oven to 230°C/Fan 210°C/Gas 8.

Mix the butter with your choice of spices and herbs, then smear all over the chicken. Place the chicken in a roasting tin, and give it a bit of extra seasoning with salt and pepper. Squeeze a little lemon over the chicken and then place the lemon halves inside.

Roast the chicken for 10–15 minutes, then turn the bird over so it is breast-side-down and reduce the oven temperature to 190°C/Fan 170°C/Gas 5. Roast for a further 30–45 minutes with occasional basting. The bird should be golden brown all over with a crisp skin, and have buttery, lemony juices of a nutty brown colour in the tin.

Turn the chicken back over to breast-side-up, switch the oven off and keep the door ajar, return the chicken to the warm oven and allow to rest for 15 minutes.

How about adding some finely chopped anchovies, mustard, grated zests, stock powder, balsamic vinegar, Tabasco, soy sauce? Not all together though!

Red-Grape Poussins with Fig, Hazelnut and Feta Stuffing

SERVES 4

4 poussins, ready for roasting

35 seedless red grapes

1 tbsp mild olive oil, plus extra
   for drizzling

½ tsp dark muscovado sugar

1 chicken stock cube

50g whole blanched hazelnuts

200g ready-made polenta,
   chopped into very small
   pieces

50g white breadcrumbs

3 fresh figs, diced

1 tsp allspice

3 tbsp extra virgin olive oil

1 egg, beaten

100g feta cheese, diced

Hazelnuts have been much loved in cookery for a long time, even appearing in Apicius' first-century cookbook in a recipe for sweets. Pairing the nut in this stuffing with allspice and figs feels festive and celebratory. It is no surprise that figs, that beautiful, velvety member of the mulberry family, have been a symbol of fertility, sweetness and abundance throughout the centuries.

Preheat the oven to 220°C/Fan 200°C/Gas 7.

Place the poussins in a roasting tin, drizzle with olive oil and cook for 45 minutes.

While they are cooking, whizz the grapes in a food processor till broken down into very small pieces. Strain and keep the red solids aside in a bowl. Mix the grape juice with the olive oil, muscovado and stock cube – using a spoon to crush the cube and mix it in as much as possible. Toast the hazelnuts in a dry pan, then pulse a few times in a food processor or break up with a pestle in a mortar until reduced to small, but not tiny, chunks.

Squeeze the polenta pieces through your fingers, like when rubbing butter through flour for crumble. Mix with the breadcrumbs, continuing to rub together for a lumpy texture. Add the hazelnuts, then the figs, allspice, extra virgin olive oil, some salt to season and a generous grinding of black pepper. Gently stir to mix, being careful not to mash up the figs too much. Add the egg and carefully mix again. Add the feta, gently combining, not stirring too much so as not to crumble.

Shape into 16 walnut-sized balls and place on an oiled baking tray. Brush the tops with olive oil. Bake towards the top of oven for the last 20 minutes of the poussin's cooking time, until golden brown and crisp.

Five minutes before the end of the cooking time, pour the grape juice and stock liquid over the birds, using a brush to blend in any remaining lumps of chicken stock. Take the grape solids that were set aside and pat and press over the poussins. Cook for the remaining 5 minutes until golden. Serve with the balls of stuffing.

You could use cranberry for the poussins, as I do at Christmas. To vary the stuffing, omit the allspice and maybe use snippets of roasted peppers.

Roasted Vegetables with Agave, Pineapple and Mint

200g baby courgettes
150g baby carrots, with tops
110g baby leeks
3 tbsp butter
1 tsp ground cumin
½ tsp dried mint
1 tbsp agave syrup or honey
1 tbsp pineapple juice

At Christmas, I often roast vegetables such as parsnips and carrots with honey and wholegrain mustard, or maple syrup, ground cumin and orange juice, so when I had a selection of baby vegetables at home, I thought I might try a similar combination with a few pieces of plain meaty monkfish. I plumped for pineapple juice to enhance the sweetness of the vegetables, with a smattering of dried mint leaf for depth, and agave nectar (a new natural sweetener) to caramelise instead of the usual honey. A sprinkle of ground cumin, with its scent of a Middle Eastern souk, provided the crucial base note, completing the harmony.

Preheat the oven to 190°C/Fan 170°C/Gas 5. Scrub and dry the vegetables. Halve the courgettes lengthways.

In a pan on a very low heat, melt the butter with the cumin, mint, agave syrup and pineapple juice, and season with salt.

Place the carrots on a baking tray, drizzle the butter mixture on top and roast for 5 minutes. Add the courgettes, rolling them in the butter mixture in the pan to coat, and roast the carrots and courgettes for 10 minutes. Turn the courgettes over, add the leeks, roll in the butter again and then roast all the vegetables for another 10 minutes.

Serve with the buttery juices drizzled on top.

Try using any fruit juice, and maybe oregano instead of the dried mint. You could also use maple syrup instead of the agave or honey.

Gremolata Rack of Lamb with Aduki Beans and Frozen Lassi

With forward planning, this is a useful supper to make after work. Once you have put the lamb to marinate in the morning and the lassi into the freezer, all that's needed is an effortless half an hour in the evening. I particularly like this during that time of the year when the weather makes tentative steps towards spring, only to keep nervously retreating into winter. This meal, with the tender, juicy lamb, is wholesome and warming, yet not too heavy.

First, make the frozen lassi (see page 209 for the recipe).

Combine the gremolata ingredients and, keeping a bit aside to scatter over at the end, rub all over the lamb. Cover and set aside for an hour.

Preheat the oven to 200°C/Fan 180°C/Gas 6.

Place the lamb racks on a baking tray and cook for 20 minutes for pink flesh, or longer if you prefer. Rest for 10 minutes and then scatter with more fresh gremolata.

Heat the butter in a pan and crumble in the stock cube. Stir well to mix, add the drained beans and heat through.

Serve with the lamb, placing a cube of the frozen lassi on top of the beans. I like the frozen lassi melting on to the beans, but you don't have to freeze it. You could add some of those flavourings to a spoonful of natural yoghurt, butter or crème fraîche, if you prefer, and you could have potatoes instead of the beans.

Gremolata is great on roast potatoes too. Use any beans or pulses in this recipe. I also like using puy lentils, simmered in a little stock and white wine. Alternatively, you could use orange or lime zest instead of lemon in the gremolata.

SERVES 2

FOR THE GREMOLATA

zest of 2 lemons

1 garlic clove, crushed
    a handful of flat-leaf parsley,
    finely chopped

sea salt

4 tbsp olive oil

FOR THE LAMB

2 racks of lamb, each 6-bone,
    French trimmed

FOR THE BEANS

1 tbsp butter

1/2 lamb stock cube

410g can of aduki beans in
    water, drained (drained weight
    is 235g)

Red Snapper Brushed with Chipotle, Strawberry and Rosé

SERVES 2

2 whole red snapper, scaled and
   gutted, washed and patted dry
oil, for greasing (I use mild olive
   oil)
1 shallot, roughly chopped

FOR THE PASTE

1 shallot, roughly chopped
6 strawberries, roughly chopped
2 tsp chipotle paste
$^1/_2$ tsp dark muscovado sugar,
   plus 1 tsp to serve
1 tbsp rosé wine, plus 2 tbsp to
   serve

Red snapper, with their head-turning beauty, look almost too ornamental to eat. On a hot day sparkling with sunshine, I grill them with a brushing of chipotle paste, which is made from dried red-ripe jalapeño chillies, and gives off the smoky, spicy scent that often dances around a Mexican barbecue, its boldness adding the perfect degree of robust warmth to the fish. Inspired by the snapper's shimmering pink scales, as exquisite as the sequins on a ballroom dancer's dress, I add a splash of summery rosé wine for moistness and some crushed fresh strawberries to complement the creamy flesh. This is not so strange an addition to the chilli, given that the strawberries we enjoy in our British summers are the descendants of those from South America.

Preheat the oven to 200°C/Fan 180°C/Gas 6 and put a baking tray inside to heat up.

Slash the fish a few times diagonally on each side.

Pulse the paste ingredients together in a food processor. Oil the baking tray, then place the snapper on it, spreading half the paste all over the top of the fish, pushing into the slashes, and setting the other half of the paste aside. Cook for 10 minutes.

Turn the fish over, spread the rest of the paste over, sprinkle each one with another half a teaspoon of muscovado and grill on high for about 3–5 minutes until golden and crisp. Splash each fish with a tablespoon of rosé before serving.

Brush the fish with fresh garlic butter, chopped parsley and sweet chilli sauce or paprika mixed with melted butter and a splash of beer.

Seared Mushrooms with Red Chilli Thari

SERVES 4

3 tbsp oil, plus extra to cook the
   mushrooms

1 tsp freshly crushed garlic

1 tsp grated fresh ginger

110g canned chopped tomatoes

1/2 tsp tandoori masala

1/2 tsp salt

1/2 tsp ground turmeric

1 1/2 red finger chillies, finely
   chopped

1/2 tsp white granulated sugar

a handful of chopped fresh
   coriander

assorted fresh mushrooms,
   whole or thickly sliced (such
   as chestnut, wild, portabella,
   shitake, enoki)

Thari simply means a relatively thin sauce in Punjabi, and so, at home, it is how we refer to a dish that has a bit of sauce, rather than a dry dish. We normally cook this type of base sauce along with the meat, fish or vegetables in the same pan. We don't cook sauces separately. I thought I'd try the idea here, just an occasional drizzle of sauce to streak some flavour across the plate but not swamp the mushrooms, so you can appreciate their flavour fully. I serve this with some simple, steamed white basmati rice, a Zen foil for the intense sauce.

Heat the oil in a pan and add the garlic and ginger. Fry, stirring continuously, until golden brown. Turn the heat down and add the rest of the ingredients, except the mushrooms. Stir well. With the heat low, stir occasionally, until the mixture becomes shiny and the oil begins to separate. Then add 120ml boiling water and stir well until you have an evenly blended sauce.

Brush a griddle pan with a little oil and sear the mushrooms, serving with the hot sauce.

Asparagus with Mustard Seed Cream

I like just a very small amount of sauce with this favourite vegetable of mine. A few weeks ago, I tried the white variety in Alsace, where it is a speciality. I have to say, I prefer our slender green tips to the chunkier, white variety, which I feel taste a lot like leek. They, in turn, are not too fond of our green ones. But I did like the sauce with which it was served in one restaurant, which was similar to this in that it was cream based. However, I have littered my crème fraîche version with black mustard seeds for some texture and a very gentle pepperiness.

Heat the oil and butter in a pan with the mustard and cumin seeds. When sizzling, add the onion and garlic, and fry, until light golden.

Turn down the heat and add the salt and garam masala. Stir well. Add the crème fraîche, stir well again and cook through for about a minute.

Brush a griddle pan with oil and cook the asparagus for a few minutes on each side, until nicely browned. Serve with a drizzle of the sauce.

This sauce is also nice with fish and/or mashed potato. I have used black, but you could use other mustard seeds, or perhaps even poppy or cumin seeds.

SERVES 4

1 tbsp olive oil, plus extra to griddle the asparagus
3 tsp butter
3 tsp black mustard seeds
1 tsp cumin seeds
1 onion, finely sliced and then chopped
1 clove of garlic, crushed
1/2 tsp salt
a pinch of garam masala
1 tub of crème fraîche, about 200ml
asparagus for 4 people

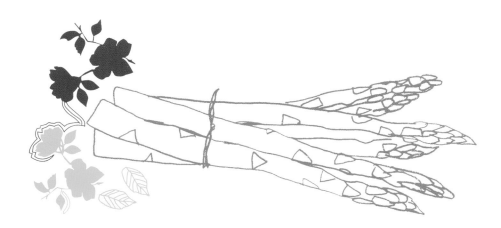

Courgettes stuffed with Coffee Rice and Oregano

SERVES 4

4 courgettes

1 tbsp butter

2 shallots, finely chopped

100g basmati rice, washed and
drained

½ chicken stock cube

2 tsp instant coffee granules

1 tsp fresh, chopped oregano,
plus extra for sprinkling

70g goat's cheese

olive oil, for drizzling

With a name like 'dirty rice' it was impossible not to try this. I came across it when flicking through a copy of *Oprah* magazine: a recipe for rice cooked with coffee grounds. What struck me was the use of oregano with the coffee. This made me want to pull out herby, green vegetable notes to contrast with the intense coffee flavour, which is why I decided to use it to stuff courgettes. I absolutely loved the results. I added a crumbling of goat's cheese on top, grilled till golden. This is one of my favourite dishes and a satisfying meal for vegetarians.

Bring a large pan of water to the boil, add the courgettes and cook for 7 minutes. Remove from the pan, allow to cool, halve lengthways, then scoop out the pulp using a spoon, without breaking the skin, to leave a shell. Set the shells and the flesh aside.

Melt the butter in a deep non-stick frying pan, add the shallots and fry until golden. Add the drained rice and stir well. Add 240ml water, the stock cube half, coffee granules and oregano. Bring to the boil, then cook, covered, on a very low heat for about 7 minutes, or until the water has absorbed and the rice is cooked. Season with a little salt and set aside to cool.

Remove the rice from the pan and use the same pan for the courgettes. Don't add any oil, just put in the courgette shells, skin-side down, and dry-fry, still over a very low heat, for a couple of minutes to brown a little. Remove and set aside on foil on a grill pan. Now add the courgette flesh to the pan and fry for about a minute and a half, stirring all the while, until it feels like the liquid has evaporated. Off the heat, add the rice and stir well.

Preheat the grill to hot.

Spoon the mixture into the courgette skins. Top each with some crumbled goat's cheese, sprinkle over a touch more oregano and a drizzle of olive oil. Place under the hot grill for about 8 minutes or until the cheese is browned.

Try the rice alone with some chicken or fish; chargrilled salmon would be particularly good. Perhaps try stuffing mushrooms instead.

Paprika and Parmesan Chicken Skewers

MAKES 2 SKEWERS

1 tsp smoked paprika
1/2 tsp tomato purée
1 tbsp extra virgin olive oil
3 tbsp freshly grated Parmesan
good squeeze of lemon juice
about 240g chicken breast fillets,
   cut lengthways into 6 strips

Complex and multifaceted, paprika is intriguing: it can be bitter and unpleasant without the persuasion of a little acidity, then the addition of some lemon, for example, encourages it to reveal a soulful warmth in the intimacy of the palate. The umami savouriness of the Parmesan is a great partner for smoky paprika, creating a richly flavoured and deep-orange coloured coating for the meat. I thread the chicken strips onto the skewer in curves 'yakitori-style', like the Japanese do. You could cook these in a pan or in the oven, if you prefer, but I like to grill or barbecue them to get them quite brown and singed at the edges.

Mix the paprika, tomato purée, olive oil, 2 tbsp of the Parmesan and the lemon juice together, then rub into the chicken. Set aside while soaking 2 wooden skewers in water for 30 minutes.

Preheat the grill to hot.

Thread 3 strips back and forth on each skewer, yakitori-style. Place under the hot grill and cook for around 15 minutes, turning regularly, until browned all over. Sprinkle with the remaining Parmesan before serving.

You could use another type of chilli, such as ground jalapeño, cayenne, piri piri or regular red chilli powder, instead of the paprika. Or you could rub the mixture over a whole chicken before roasting.

Mirin Mackerel with Brown Rice and Spring Onion

This is as balanced, nutritious and wholesome as it is delicious, and it's a perfect light lunch or snack, as good cold as it is hot. It is often in my fridge when I am on a rare exercise regime, when I make batches to stave off chocolate-bar cravings. To be fully virtuous, omit the mirin and soak in a little miso soup or paste instead. However, the mirin-soaked mackerel goes perfectly with the nutty, chewy, filling brown rice and the slight sharpness of the spring onion, with the splash of salty soy pulling it all together and teasing its way into the rice when kept in the fridge for a little while.

Pour a tablespoon of mirin over each of the fillets and then sprinkle over a teaspoon of the sugar and massage in. Leave to marinate for an hour, covered.

Place under a hot grill for 10 minutes until the top has caramelised. Flake into small pieces.

Mix the rice with the spring onions and add a good few dashes of soy sauce. Add the mackerel pieces and mix together with a fork.

SERVES 2

2 tbsp mirin

2 smoked mackerel fillets, skin removed

2 tsp dark muscovado sugar

½ mugful brown rice, cooked (wash thoroughly, add 1 mugful water, bring to the boil and simmer until cooked through but al dente, adding more water if necessary)

3 spring onions, finely sliced

soy sauce

Grilled Sardines with Beetroot, Pink Grapefruit and Parsley

SERVES 2

4 sardines, scaled and gutted, cleaned and patted dry

olive oil, for brushing

flaked sea salt and cracked black pepper

1 pink grapefruit, in segments

250g cooked beetroot, chopped

a small handful of fresh parsley, chopped

1/2 tsp cumin seeds, toasted in a dry pan and then smashed up a bit with a pestle in a mortar to release the aromas

3 tbsp orange-blossom water

3 tsp honey

A colourful dish, this is infused with the flavour of Moorish southern Spain. The orange-blossom water brings Andalusian charm to the beetroot, grapefruit and parsley, pulling these diverse flavours together with its floral fragrance. If you haven't already tried it, this perfumed ingredient is well worth keeping in your store cupboard. A sprinkling on fresh strawberries is divine.

I try to use parsley more as a flavouring than the garnish it is often relegated to. It's a herb we should celebrate. After all, the Ancient Greeks considered it sacred. According to legend, parsley sprang up where the blood of Archemorus was spilled when he was eaten by serpents. The Greeks also made parsley wreaths to crown their winning athletes and to adorn graves. The Hebrew celebration of Passover uses the herb as a symbol of spring and rebirth. In Christianity, it was associated with the Apostle Peter, warder of the gates of heaven.

Flat-leaf parsley took a little while to catch on as an ingredient. The fact that it was sometimes mistaken for the poisonous weed 'fool's-parsley' probably didn't help. And some medieval farmers were afraid to grow it, believing that the long germination period for the seeds was because they travelled to hell and back seven times before sprouting.

Slash each sardine 3 times on each side, brush with olive oil, season with flaked sea salt and cracked pepper and place under a medium grill for about 5 minutes on each side. Brush with more oil and season again when you turn them over.

Place the grapefruit, beetroot and parsley on the serving plate. Mix together the cumin, orange-blossom water and honey and pour over the salad. Serve with the hot sardines.

Try other fish such as mackerel. You could also use white grapefruit, or orange or blood-orange segments instead of the grapefruit. Also, try flavouring white sauces with parsley stalks, removing before serving so you get the flavour without the green colour.

AFTER

There have been more occasions than I perhaps should mention when I have been so enthusiastic and impatient for dessert that I have promptly reversed the order of my meal, beginning with something sweet instead, and sometimes remaining there in a sugary bliss. However, as 'afters' are generally eaten after a meal, I have placed the puddings here in this section.

I tend to think of sweet treats in terms of the temperature at which they are served and thus how they complement the rest of the meal, the seasons and your own mood. Some are light and refreshing and some are pure indulgence. They range from cubes of fruity Mango Ice which can be generously piled onto platters and shared with Dipping Sugar and chattering friends at a summer party to pillows of piping hot Sweet Potato Fritti you can pile into a bowl and share with nothing but the spoon and your mouth whilst curled up on the sofa and wrapped in the cosiest blanket.

ICED

Masala Chai Ices
Mandarin, Basil and Lime Sorbet
White Pears on Black Ice
Mango Ice Sticks with Dipping Sugar
White Grape and Bay Parfait
Turkish Delight Chocolate Ice Cream Drops
White Chocolate, Coconut and Redcurrant Messy Sundaes

COLD

Green Raisin, Sherbet Lemon and Ginger Cheesecake
Starfruit with Jalapeño and Palm Sugar Yoghurt
Blackberries in Earl Grey with Cashew Nut Ice Cream
Elderflower Jellies with Papaya
Mango Toffee Roulade
Lime, Coconut and Mint Mousse Shots
Honey Melon Creams
Cardamom Chocolate Pots
Apricot Cinnamon Fudge with Chocolate Chips

WARM

Green Tea Butterfly Cakes with Honeycomb Cream
Pecan and Date Caramel Tartlets
Passionfruit and White Chocolate Oat Cookies
Rhubarb and Rosewater Fairy Cakes
Chilli and Pomegranate Chocolate Brownies

HOT

Sweet Potato Cinnamon Fritti with Sour Cherry Syrup and Clove
    Maple Ice Cream
Hibiscus Berry Soup with Lemongrass Boudoir Biscuits
Sesame and Coconut Cookies with Lemon Thyme Dipping Sauce
Chargrilled Pineapple with Salted Caramel

Masala Chai Ices

MAKES 4 ICE LOLLIES

4 green cardamom pods,
   cracked
1 brown cardamom pod, cracked
4 cloves
¼ tsp fennel seeds
¼ tsp ground ginger
1 stick of cinnamon
2 tbsp sugar
1 tea bag (of your choice)

These refreshing ice lollies flavoured with cardamom, clove, fennel, ginger and cinnamon are a huge hit with my friends. I originally created the recipe for the excellent charity Railway Children, who help vulnerable children at railway stations the world over. Thinking of the ubiquitous sight of chai-wallahs carrying steel pots of tea and pouring long, hot streams into glasses in stations and on trains all over India, I came up with these ices made from black tea spiced with all the aromas of Indian chai.

Bring 450ml water to the boil in a pan over a medium heat with all the ingredients except for the tea bag, stirring to dissolve the sugar. Once boiling, add the tea bag and simmer for a couple of minutes.

Strain into a jug and leave to cool. Stir well, pour into moulds and freeze: use lolly moulds or shot glasses with wooden sticks.

Try with just cardamom or ginger, or a black tea with lemon version. You could also freeze this in an ice cube tray, then whizz in a food processor to make a granita.

Mandarin, Basil and Lime Sorbet

SERVES 8

3 x 298g cans of mandarin
   segments in juice, drained
   (drained weight of each can
   is 175g)
zest of 2 limes and 2 tbsp lime
   juice
1 tbsp finely chopped basil
   leaves
140g white granulated sugar

This was inspired by the delicious Jo Malone fragrance, which combines the same scents. I find this dessert just perfect for summer and I often serve it quite roughly, more like a granita, in little cups or piled into small cones. Remember, the mixture will taste very sweet before you freeze it, as the freezing process dulls the sweetness of the sugar.

Blend the mandarin segments in a food processor and then strain to give 300ml juice. Stir in the lime zest and juice and the basil.

Place the sugar in a saucepan with 270ml water and, over a low heat, stir every so often until the sugar has dissolved. Turn the heat up to bring the syrup to the boil and boil for 1 minute without stirring. Allow to cool for about 5 minutes.

Add the syrup to the other ingredients in a shallow container. Allow to cool, then transfer to the freezer. Allow to freeze for around 5 hours, scraping the sides into the unfrozen centre with a fork around every hour.

Blackcurrant, vanilla and mint leaf would be a nice alternative.

White Pears on Black Ice

OK, so this is more like pale beige pears on dark brown ice, but I think you'll agree that that doesn't have quite the same ring to it, so I hope you will forgive me. I know that some people put almond milk in their coffee, and that led me to wonder about the combination of coconut cream with coffee, which I first thought would be odd, and was then intrigued by. This is an unusual dessert: pears poached in coconut milk and served on top of coffee granita. It was unfamiliar to the taste buds for the first couple of mouthfuls and then I really liked it a lot. I wanted to give the buttery texture of the pear (which Homer called the 'gift of the gods to humanity') an exotic treatment. It seems the Romans ate pears in a similar way, stewing them, never eating them raw.

Mix together the water, coffee and sugar until dissolved, then freeze in an ice cube tray.

Place the sugar in a pan with the coconut milk but not the coconut cream. Heat on a low heat until the sugar has dissolved. When simmering, add the pears. Cover with a lid and simmer for about 15 minutes or until tender. Remove the pears from the liquid and set aside to cool. When cooled, use a corer to remove the centre of the pears, and chill them. Freeze the poaching liquid in ice cubes to make a different granita, if you like, or else discard.

Blitz the ice cubes in a food processor. Place a pear on top and then drizzle over some of the coconut cream.

It doesn't matter if the pears float in the pan of milk or stand upright, as long as they have enough space to cook through. Perhaps poach the pears in sugar syrup and serve over lemon or elderflower granita.

SERVES 4

500ml hot water
8 tsp instant coffee granules
4 tbsp caster sugar

FOR THE PEARS

300g caster sugar
800ml coconut milk
4 pears, peeled but with stalk and any leaves still on, a sliver cut from the base so they stand up
100ml coconut cream

Mango Ice Sticks with Dipping Sugar

MAKES ABOUT 12 CUBES

2 very ripe mangoes, about 375g flesh (I use Indian mangoes with a deep orange flesh)

FOR THE DIPPING SUGAR

1 tbsp light muscovado sugar

1 tbsp white sugar

1 tbsp coarse sea salt

zest of 1 lemon

zest of 1 lime

couple of good pinches of cayenne pepper

Sometimes I like to do very informal desserts, something fun that people can dip into and share while chatting away. This is very simple, just mango flesh puréed and frozen in cubes with sticks like little ice lollies. It is the dipping sugar that makes it grown up. A complex mix of sweet, sour, salt and even a little chilli heat, it is strong, so a little on the edge of your ice is all it needs to lift the fruity sweetness to new heights. I've used light muscovado sugar as it is not too dense but also has a toffee-like character. It's important to mix this just as you are about to serve or it will melt and the colours and flavours will bleed into each other, which you don't want.

Purée the mango flesh in a food processor or blender, pour into an ice cube tray and freeze. When semi-frozen, insert cocktail sticks into each cube.

Gently mix all the dipping sugar ingredients just before serving. Turn the mango cubes out and serve with a bowl of the dipping sugar.

Make these with any fruit you like, or a mixture of fruits. You could try a smoothie-like blend, such as bananas or strawberries with some cream or coconut.

White Grape and Bay Parfait

SERVES 6–8

500ml double cream

5 egg yolks

90g caster sugar

1 bay leaf

30 white grapes, cut lengthways
  into about 4 slices each

115ml white grape juice

$\frac{1}{2}$ tsp ground bay leaf

There is something about this that feels so elegant and refined, almost like an Edwardian English lady. This is probably no surprise given that I made it the day after I had seen *The Wings of the Dove*. This is cool, clean and precise, with a little green crystal embellishment from the studding of grapes and a whisper of bohemian spice from the bay. When I tried it, I felt like it needed to be eaten in complete silence, a neat slice on a china plate, perfectly poised. Ground bay leaf is utterly essential here, following the tradition of using bay in milk puddings in Britain since the days of the Tudors. The ground leaf is not available in all supermarkets but you can get it online, so this is something to save for, and savour.

Whip the cream until thickened and just about holding its shape. Whisk the egg yolks with an electric mixer until pale.

Place the caster sugar and 3 tablespoons of water in a pan with the bay leaf and dissolve the sugar over a low heat, stirring to help it do so. Once the sugar has dissolved, bring to the boil, then simmer for 3 minutes without stirring. Remove the bay leaf.

Whisking with the mixer on medium speed the whole time, slowly add the hot sugar syrup (be careful not to get sugar syrup on the beaters or the base of the bowl as it will stick) to the egg yolks, then lower the speed and continue to whisk for another 5 minutes. Fold this mixture into the cream, then fold in the grapes, grape juice and ground bay leaf. Gently stir to mix evenly and pour into a 900g loaf tin lined with cling film.

Freeze overnight. Place in the fridge for about 15 minutes before serving to soften for slicing.

You could use the basic parfait recipe and try other flavours, such as peach and raspberry, or orange with dark chocolate chunks.

Turkish Delight Chocolate Ice Cream Drops

This is really just me playing around with ice cream and trying different ways to make it a little more interesting as a dessert, looking at textures and temperatures and ways of combining and serving individual components. At the Japanese restaurant Nobu, there is something similar to this, where balls of ice cream are coated in cake crumbs and then deep-fried till hot and crisp on the outside, and creamy and still frozen on the inside. They make something similar in Mexico, too, using cornmeal or flakes to encrust the chilly centre. I will try that as well, but in the meantime, these are sort of ice cream truffles: chocolate ice-cream balls encasing a single bite of Turkish delight, then wrapped in cake crumbs.

I made them because I love Turkish delight, but I like it best when it is really cold from the fridge. This is pretty inauthentic, but I can't help it. I also very much like Cadbury's chocolate-covered version, though I know it is sweeter and so much less delicate than the traditional rose or lemon-scented varieties. There are many myths surrounding the origin of true Turkish delight. One is that a sultan ordered his chefs to create a dessert with which to woo his mistresses. Another is that it was created by confectioner Bekir Effendi in the eighteenth century, who came from high up in the Anatolian mountains to Istanbul to set up the shop where the tender sweet was born. The shop still stands to this day.

Allow the ice cream to soften slightly, then scoop up balls using a melon-baller. Quickly shape each ball of ice cream round a piece of Turkish delight, then roll in the cake crumbs. Place on a tray and refreeze until needed.

Use this technique to try any other flavours – perhaps mix some grated red apple flesh into vanilla ice cream and place a piece of fudge or soft toffee in the centre, coating with madeira cake crumbs.

MAKES 12

500ml tub of chocolate ice cream (or to make your own, see page 207), from which you take 12 scoops

2 Cadbury's Turkish Delight bars, each cut into 6 pieces

200g madeira or chocolate cake, whizzed to crumbs

White Chocolate, Coconut and Redcurrant Messy Sundaes

MAKES 6

250g redcurrants, plus a few extra sprigs for decoration

1 tbsp caster sugar

100g coconut flakes

500ml white chocolate ice cream (or you can make your own – see page 208)

3 meringues, crushed

100ml coconut cream

50g white chocolate, shaved with a peeler

Originally I tried to make this as a layered iced terrine dessert, not dissimilar to that old classic, Wall's Viennetta. Then I became impatient and decided to eat it like this instead, a combination of an ice cream sundae and Eton mess, just layer piled upon layer of a few of my favourite things. I use precious garnet redcurrants, which are perfect for birthdays. The exotic creaminess does make this a sundae for grown-ups, I think to myself, spoon in mouth, noticing a few stray post-birthday balloons which, three months later, still bob around by the fireplace.

Strip the berries from their stalks with a fork, then pulse them in a food processor with the sugar, just to crush, not to purée them.

In glasses, layer the ingredients, finishing with white chocolate shavings and a sprig of berries.

THE COCONUT PALM is known as the tree that grants all wishes. Native to the Pacific, the buoyant seed spread throughout South Asia on ocean currents. Coconut became a part of many Indian rituals and ceremonies, with early Sanskrit literature featuring it from the fourth century BC. It played the role of an offering, cracked open, spilling its contents, replacing the animal sacrifices that were forbidden when India became vegetarian, King Ashoka having witnessed so much war and bloodshed that it gave him frenzied fevers.

Green Raisin, Sherbet Lemon and Ginger Cheesecake

SERVES 8–10

25g unsalted butter, softened

25g breadcrumbs

1 tsp ground ginger

225g golden caster sugar, plus
1 tsp for the base

700g full-fat cream cheese

2 eggs

350ml whipping cream

40g plain flour, sifted

75g raisins (I am using green
raisins)

4 sherbet lemons

a few pieces of crystallised ginger

This is a proper New York baked cheesecake, adapted from a recipe from Annie Bell. The cream cheese mixture, even before you bake it, is divine. As is the sight of the golden top, puffing its way out of the tin when it is cooked. I had some green raisins left over, so I used those. We use this smaller, subtly sweet variety a lot in Indian cooking and tea, but you can use regular raisins. If you can, turn off the fan setting of your oven, as Annie recommends. Also, cover with foil when cooling, not clingfilm, or it will go soggy.

Sherbet lemons are a delightful retro treat. I buy a bag with infantile glee, eat half on the way home and then crush up the rest to make a topping of acid-sweet gems and crystallised ginger.

Preheat the oven to 200°C/Fan 180°C/Gas 6. (The non-fan setting is preferable.)

Use all the butter to grease the insides of a 20cm springform cake tin, 7cm deep. Mix the breadcrumbs with the ginger and 1 teaspoon of sugar. Press the breadcrumb mixture into the base and sides of the tin.

Place the 225g of sugar and the cream cheese in a food processor and whizz until smooth. Add the eggs and cream and blend well, then fold in the flour and stir in the raisins. Pour into the cake tin and bake in the centre of the oven for 45 minutes. Cover very loosely with foil after 30 minutes so it doesn't get too brown. It should be golden brown and puffy but still have a distinct wobble.

Turn the oven off and leave the door ajar, allowing the cheesecake to cool down gradually for an hour. Then cover loosely with foil and chill overnight.

Allow the cheesecake about 30 minutes to come back to room temperature. In the meantime, place the sherbet lemons in a food bag, bash with a rolling pin, empty out into a food processor and whizz until crystals. Be careful to cover the food chute with your hand or crystals will come flying out.

Release the cake from the springform tin. Use a sharp knife to score all around the edge of the bottom of the cheesecake to ease it from the base. Use a fish slice to gently ease it on to a plate.

Sprinkle the top of the cheesecake with the sherbet lemon crystals just before serving, and chop the crystallised ginger into small pieces and scatter these on top too.

Why not try omitting the ginger from the base, add a few chopped cherries instead of the raisins to the filling, then top with more fresh cherries, stalks on. Or how about an orange and ginger variety with ground ginger in the base, orange juice in the filling and candied orange slices on top?

Starfruit with Jalapeño and Palm Sugar Yoghurt

SERVES 2

3 tbsp Greek yoghurt

2 slices jalapeño, rinsed, deseeded and very finely chopped

1 tsp granulated palm sugar

1 starfruit, very thinly sliced

Very quick, very simple. Generally speaking, the starfruit eaten alone can seem a bit sterile and frigid. It's neither sweet nor tender. But sliced, its cool, crisp glassiness is refreshing with the yoghurt. The little flakes of jalapeño pepper seem to pull out the fruit's hidden juiciness and the caramel flavour of the palm sugar gives it a warm sweetness. Use brown sugar if you can't find palm sugar. I found mine in the Thai section of my supermarket, in the world food aisle. You could also use a touch of finely grated jaggery, if you live near an Indian store. A Caribbean store might also have something similar.

Combine the yoghurt with the jalapeño and sugar. Serve the starfruit with the cold yoghurt mixture. And that's all there is to it.

Try with another fruit, such as pear, honeydew melon or Sharon fruit slices. You can also try drizzling the dessert with a little maple syrup instead of using the palm sugar, or try some dark muscovado instead.

Blackberries in Earl Grey with Cashew Nut Ice Cream

This is a simple but sophisticated dessert, good for a dinner party. You can make the components beforehand and assemble them later for your guests. Finger-staining, onyx blackberries are always a treat, and I thought it might be nice to steep Earl Grey tea leaves in a syrup, as I am a fan of smoky bergamot.

Instead of making the ice cream from scratch, I usually cheat somewhat for a fantastically quick version, slightly softening an excellent quality shop-bought vanilla ice cream as a base, stirring in my ingredients, then refreezing. I decided to heap broken creamy cashew nuts into the ice cream for this, recalling an unforgettable scoop I once had in Florence, the best I have ever tasted.

SERVES 6

150g golden caster sugar
2 tbsp Earl Grey tea leaves
200g cashew nuts, crushed in a
    food processor or bashed with
    a rolling pin in a food bag
300ml vanilla ice cream,
    softened (see page 208)
blackberries for 6 people

Heat the sugar in a pan with 300ml water over a low heat, stirring occasionally to help the sugar dissolve. When dissolved, turn up the heat and boil for 5 minutes without stirring. Switch off the heat, allow to cool slightly for a minute, then add the tea leaves. Steep for 5 minutes, strain and cool. Then chill in the fridge.

Mix the broken cashews into the softened vanilla ice cream, place in a container and refreeze until firm.

Serve the blackberries with the syrup spooned over them and a spoonful of the ice cream.

Try this with other berries, such as redcurrants or blackberries. Also, try adding other flavours into a vanilla ice cream base and refreezing.

Elderflower Jellies with Papaya

SERVES 4

4 gelatine leaves

600ml sparkling elderflower
    pressé, plus a few extra
    splashes to serve

1 papaya, seeds scooped out,
    cut into long slivers

A simple, light, refreshing dessert with a floral bouquet. I like serving this in glass cups, with a few tall slivers of the fruit propped up by ripples of the broken, fragrant jelly, bubbles of the pressé bursting over the top like a geyser. It is excellent for summer parties and afternoon lunches.

Soak the gelatine leaves in cold water for 15 minutes (or 5 minutes, if using the quick-dissolving variety).

Heat 150ml of the pressé until just simmering in a pan. Remove the gelatine leaves from the water, squeeze off excess liquid, then whisk into the hot pressé. Whisk in the remaining pressé. Pour into a bowl, cool and refrigerate overnight or until fully set.

Prop up some papaya slivers in tumbler glasses. Run a sharp knife through the jelly to break it up into a sort of crushed jelly. Spoon into the glasses with the papaya, and top with another splash of pressé just before serving.

Try with other fruits and jellies — how about Champagne or rose jelly? And try strips of mango or melon.

Mango Toffee Roulade

SERVES 8

butter, for greasing
6 large eggs, separated
100g light brown soft sugar
5 tbsp dulce de leche
100g plain flour, sifted
125g caster sugar, plus extra for
    dusting
200ml double cream
1 mango, cut into small chunks
icing sugar, to serve

If you're feeling a little out of sorts, sometimes cake can work little miracles. Particularly a thoroughly indulgent one, like this mango roulade. I came across a recipe for praline the other day. I decided to try the mixture without the nuts, just clear caramel instead. When you pour the sticky mixture on to the paper, you can't imagine it setting into a hard, brittle layer in just 15 minutes. But peel away the amber pane, like a stained-glass window panel, and it is thoroughly satisfying, as is snapping it like an old record and blitzing it to shards in a food processor, which always makes me feel immensely better.

Preheat the oven to 180°C/Fan 160°C/Gas 4. Grease and line the base and sides of a Swiss roll tin (about 22cm x 32cm) with baking paper.

Put the egg yolks and sugar into a large bowl. Using an electric hand-whisk, whisk for about 3 minutes until pale, thick and creamy. Whisk 2 tablespoons of the dulce de leche. Add the flour and beat in.

In a separate bowl, whisk the egg whites to soft peaks. Gently fold the egg whites into the yolk mixture using a large metal spoon until just combined. Pour into the lined tin and smooth out to the edges to fill. Bake for about 25 minutes until spongy to the touch.

Place a sheet of baking paper on the work surface and dust thickly with caster sugar. Cool the sponge for 10 minutes, then turn out on to the paper. Peel off the baking paper backing from the roulade, then cover with a clean sheet of baking paper and a damp tea towel. Leave for an hour to cool.

Meanwhile, make the filling.

For the toffee shards, line a baking sheet with baking paper, then place the caster sugar in a heavy-based pan with 2 tablespoons of water and dissolve over a low heat. Once dissolved, turn up the heat and boil, but do not stir, until the syrup begins to caramelise. When it is a deep amber colour, pour on to the baking paper in a thin layer. Leave to set for about 15 minutes. Carefully peel the amber pane off the paper, break into chunks and then crush in a food processor to give smaller shards. Whip the cream until it just holds its shape.

Trim the edges of the roulade, spread with the remaining 3 tablespoons of dulce de leche, then the whipped cream, the mango chunks and the toffee shards. Put less cream and filling on the side of the roulade furthest away from you so it doesn't all splodge out when you roll it up. Roll up the sponge tightly, using the paper to help you. Transfer to a flat serving plate. Dust thickly with sieved icing sugar or drizzle with more dulce de leche.

You can make all sorts of roulades, with different flavour sponges and fillings. What about a chocolate or a vanilla sponge? Also, don't just save your dulce de leche for cooking, try it with some fresh cut peaches and a dash of cream.

MANGOES. originating in northeast India, are part of Buddhist legend. It is said that the Buddha caused a pure white mango tree to sprout from the ground where he planted a mango stone and ran water over his hands.

Lime, Coconut and Mint Mousse Shots

MAKES 16

juice and zest of 3 limes (you
   won't use all the juice)
2 tsp powdered gelatine
3 tbsp Malibu
3 eggs
45g caster sugar
150ml whipping cream
1 tbsp chopped fresh mint
crumbled brown sugar and
   white chocolate shavings,
   to serve

We would make lemon mousse with my mother when we were little. I used to grate the zest, and our mousse would be so much more vibrant than the ready-made ones in plastic pots. It is not difficult to make this dessert, but you need to have everything ready beforehand as timing is quite crucial, and so a little preparation will go a long way.

Put a tablespoon of lime juice into a saucepan, sprinkle the gelatine over and let it stand for 5 minutes. Then add the Malibu and heat over a low heat for a couple of minutes, stirring until the gelatine is dissolved. Switch the heat off and allow to cool slightly.

Using an electric hand-whisk, whisk the eggs and sugar in a heatproof bowl set over a pan of simmering water for about 3 minutes until pale and the beaters leave a ribbon-like trail when lifted. Remove from the heat and continue to whisk until the bowl is cool to the touch.

Fold the gelatine mixture into the eggs, then place the bowl in a cold bain-marie (another dish or bowl filled with cold water and ice). Stir every so often with a large metal spoon in a figure-of-eight shape until it is just beginning to set.

Whip the cream until it holds its shape, stir in the lime zest and chopped mint, then fold into the egg mixture with a metal spoon.

Spoon into the shot glasses and leave to set in the fridge for at least an hour, topping with crumbled brown sugar and white chocolate shavings.

If you prefer, you could use some coconut syrup (for coffee) instead of the Malibu, or omit it altogether.

MINT LEAF, originating in Europe and the Mediterranean, has long been regarded as a symbol of hospitality, strewn around banquets and feasts by the Romans. Greek legend has it that two travelling strangers were snubbed by a village and offered no welcome. Then an old couple invited them inside their home for a meal, rubbing their table with fresh mint to clean and freshen it for their guests. A prudent move, as these travelling strangers turned out to be the gods Zeus and Hermes in disguise. In return for the hospitality, the Gods turned their modest home into a temple.

Honey Melon Creams

MAKES 6

430g honeydew melon flesh,
deseeded of course (the flesh
of an average-size melon)

45g sugar

8 gelatine leaves

225ml double cream, plus 150ml
extra for serving

honey, for drizzling

I serve these pannacotta-like creams in the glass ramekins or teacups in which I set them, as they are a little looser than the Italian dessert they are based on. I love their pale green colour and refreshing, quivering silkiness. Given that the dessert is made with honeydew melon, it seemed silly not to be inspired by the name and serve it with a drop of this 'food of the gods', for this is how honey was known to the Ancient Greeks. An ambrosia fed to Zeus throughout his upbringing.

Whizz the melon flesh to a purée using a food processor or blender. Pour through a strainer and squeeze as much liquid as you can out of the solids, pushing with a spoon. Place the crushed melon solids in a bowl and chill. You should now have about 270ml juice.

Take 60ml of the juice and put it in a pan. Pour the rest of the juice back into the food processor or blender and whizz with the sugar.

Soak the gelatine leaves in cold water for 15 minutes (or 5 minutes, if using the quick-dissolving variety), then squeeze out excess water. Set the pan with the juice over a low heat and, when just simmering, whisk in the gelatine until dissolved. Remove from the heat.

Place the cream in a separate pan and gently heat, stirring so it doesn't stick, till almost simmering, then remove from heat. Whisk in the gelatine juice thoroughly, and then the melon juice and sugar mixture. Allow it to cool slightly before whisking again and pouring into serving ramekins.

Chill for 8 hours or, better, overnight. Whip the remaining cream and serve the melon creams with a spoonful of this, a spoonful of the crushed cold melon and a drizzle of honey.

Try making this with raspberry or peach or kiwi. Or maybe a strawberry version with just a hint of chilli or black pepper. Whizz up any leftover melon flesh with some coconut cream and serve over ice in little cups as a cold sweet soup, or fry with some prawns, chilli and ginger for a hot salad.

SINCE THE EARLIEST civilisations, we have been helping ourselves to the sweet nectar of bee colonies. In Spain, cave paintings from 7000 BC depict beekeeping. The creation of honey is older than humanity, with fossils dating back over 150 million years.

Cardamom Chocolate Pots

We don't have much of a tradition of making Indian desserts in my family. Generally we buy them in. Thus I was a little nervous when I started trying to make puddings. This was an early success for me, one of the first ones I made, very simple but also one most people will enjoy, given how much we all love chocolate. I added a little crushed cardamom, its fragrance and gingery-warmth infusing the chocolate to make quite dense little pots of pleasure.

Gently heat the cream in a small saucepan over a low heat. When it reaches simmering point, remove from the heat and add the chocolate, stirring vigorously until completely dissolved.

Crush the cardamom pods to reveal the seeds, then discard the husks and grind the seeds in a mortar with a pestle. Add the crushed seeds to the cream and chocolate mixture, then beat in the egg yolks and mascarpone. Divide between 8 small glasses and chill for at least 3 hours.

You could make these with ground ginger instead, or cinnamon.

SERVES 8

284ml single cream
200g dark chocolate, chopped
3 cardamom pods
2 egg yolks
160g mascarpone

CARDAMOM is a flavour a lot of people associate with Indian cookery. The plants grow wild in parts of the monsoon forests of southern India, in an area known as the Cardamom Hills. The spice has been cultivated only in the last 200 years, but the wild variety has been traded for at least a thousand. With black pepper as the King, it was long known as the Queen of Spices.

Apricot Cinnamon Fudge with Chocolate Chips

I originally made this to smash up and crumble over ice cream. Adding the cinnamon was a nod to a long European tradition of adding the spice to candies, an ingredient much fought over. I can understand the fervour – the distinctive aroma certainly leaves an impression. I can only imagine the intensity of the air when the Roman emperor Nero, in a symbolic action of remorse, ordered a year's supply of the spice to be burned on the funeral pyre of the wife he murdered.

MAKES ABOUT 42 CHUNKS
mild olive oil, for greasing
300ml whole milk
300g caster sugar
100g unsalted butter
½ tsp ground cinnamon
250g chopped dried apricots
70g dark chocolate chips

Brush an 18cm square cake tin with oil.

Place the milk, sugar and butter in a heavy-based saucepan. Gently heat, stirring throughout, until the sugar has dissolved and the butter melted. When the sugar has melted, bring to the boil and boil for 15–20 minutes, stirring constantly. As you do so, wear an oven glove, use a long-handled spoon and stand back from the hot, bubbling mixture. When the mixture reaches the soft-ball stage (115°C on a sugar thermometer), remove from the heat and stir in the cinnamon and apricots. Leave to cool for 5 minutes.

Beat the mixture with a wooden spoon for a few minutes until it starts to thicken and the gloss disappears. Pour into the prepared tin and leave at room temperature (do not put it in the fridge).

When lukewarm to the touch (not warm or the chips will melt), scatter the chocolate chips over the top and press in lightly, then leave to cool and set fully.

Once it is set, cut the fudge into small squares and store them in a sealed container.

Perhaps try this fudge with other fruits, such as dates, or substitute vanilla for the cinnamon.

CINNAMON IS NATIVE to Sri Lanka (then Ceylon), traded by the Portuguese until the 17th-century Dutch seized it from them. When the Dutch discovered there was another source of cinnamon further along the coast, they initially bribed then threatened the king of that area, trying to hold on to their mono-poly. France took control of this bewitching spice during the Revolutionary Wars, with England taking over in 1795. But by 1833, cinnamon was growing in destinations such as Java and Ghana, and so the obsession over a monopoly gradually died away.

Green Tea Butterfly Cakes with Honeycomb Cream

MAKES 12

125g unsalted butter, softened

125g sugar

2 eggs

125g plain flour, sifted

1/2 tsp bicarbonate of soda

1 tsp baking powder

1/4 tsp green tea powder

1/4 tsp vanilla extract

284ml double cream, whipped till it holds stiff peaks

100g honeycomb, bashed into pieces (either in a food bag with a rolling pin, or in a food processor)

This is an adaptation of the wonderful Nigella Lawson recipe for butterfly cakes, with the addition of a little green tea flavouring and some honeycomb cream.

I came across some concentrated green tea powder in my local Japanese store and was inspired by the way they use it to flavour sweets, such as ice cream and jellies. I admit the powder is not easy to get hold of, but, once you do, a small pot will last you a long time as you only need a pinch, so strong is its distinct flavour. Opening my box reminded me of Russian dolls. Inside I found a tub, took off its lid to find a ring-pull can, opened that to find a bag folded down like a concertina, eventually working my way in to be rewarded with a small puff of green dust, like a little genie in a lamp. I liked the idea of baking something as innocent as butterfly cakes but making them mysterious with the unusual, faintly bitter flavour of green tea, tinting the sponge the colour of a pale jade bracelet.

With the green tea making the sponge almost savoury and serene, I added a few nuggets of sweet gold in the cream filling to balance the flavour out. I could eat honeycomb, or 'hokey pokey', till my teeth fall out. I refer you to Nigella's delicious recipe if you want to make it from scratch. However, mine comes as ready-bought lumps, like mineral ore, in a pastel-striped box, ready to smash. I add it to the cream only as I am about to serve, or it will start to dissolve, and it is nice to have some discernible toothsome crunch. With a little spoonful on top and the wings balanced on it, these cakes are demurely enticing.

Preheat the oven to 200°C/Fan 180°C/Gas 6, and line a 12-bun muffin tin with cases.

Cream the butter and sugar in a bowl by hand or with an electric mixer. Once it is, well, creamy, and light and fluffy, add the eggs one at a time with a little of the flour, beating as you go. Fold in the rest of the flour, sift in the bicarbonate of soda and baking powder, then add the green tea powder and vanilla extract and stir well.

Spoon the batter into the muffin cases, dividing equally. Place in the oven for 15–20 minutes or until they are golden on top and springy to the touch. Allow to cool in the cases for 5 minutes, then carefully remove from the cases and cool fully on a wire rack.

Cut off the peak on the top or dig out a disc and cut in half. Combine the cream with the honeycomb and put a dollop on each cake, sticking the cake halves to it like wings.

Try adding other flavours to the sponge, such as coffee, and drop some chocolate chips into the cream.

Pecan and Date Caramel Tartlets

MAKES 4

caramel (see page 208)

4 frozen shortcrust tartlet cases
(from 366g pack of 6)

60ml double cream

1 tbsp orange blossom water

200g pecan nuts, lightly toasted
in a dry non-stick pan

100g dates, chopped

Piled generously high, these are sweet and indulgent. Serve half a tartlet with vanilla ice cream, or crème fraîche with a bit of lime zest and some dark chocolate shavings to cut through the sweetness. The tartlets have quite a rich, autumnal flavour and go well with steaming cups of coffee, perfect for sitting around the fireplace and gossiping with friends after supper.

First, make the caramel. This recipe can be found on page 208. Preheat the oven and a baking tray to 200°C/Fan 180°C/Gas 6.

Take one of the tartlet cases out of its box and remove its paper case. Pull out a length of baking paper, cut, fold in half and then half again. On the top layer, trace around the paper case, then draw a circle around it about 1cm bigger. Cut this out and you will have 4 sheets. Use these to line the frozen cases, then fill with baking beans, place on the preheated tray and cook for 15 minutes. Remove the paper and beans and return the tartlet cases to the oven for 5–7 minutes or until golden brown. Remove and cool.

Set the pan with the caramel in over a very low heat to soften, then stir in the double cream, melting it into the caramel. When smooth, add the orange-blossom water. Tip in the nuts and dates, stir to coat well, switch off the heat and allow to cool a little. Pile the cases high with the mixture.

Omit the dates and use figs instead, or use walnuts or hazelnuts instead of pecans. You could add a few broken chunks of dark chocolate, stirring it in when the caramel is cold, otherwise it will melt. A delicious combination is pecan and chocolate tartlets with orange zest.

Passionfruit and White Chocolate Oat Cookies

These tropical cookies are large, soft and chewy. I had wanted to make a cookie with the rustic texture of oats, but with an exotic juicy sweetness, some crunch and a murmur of tang. The passionfruit obliged on all three counts. These are easy to make but impressive. This recipe makes a lot but they are great to give away to friends, especially if they need cheering up. One recipient did not believe I had made them, insisting they must have been shop-bought. I hope this is a compliment.

Preheat the oven to 190°C/Fan 170°C/Gas 5.

In a bowl, cream together the butter and both sugars until well-mixed and smooth. This is easiest done with an electric whisk. Add the flour, bicarbonate of soda and salt, stirring in until well mixed. Add the oats and mix in until the whole thing looks like lumpy breadcrumbs. Stir in the passionfruit and then slowly mix in the egg. Gently stir in the chocolate, just enough to combine.

Place dollops about the size of large walnuts on baking trays lined with baking parchment, and flatten slightly. Leave at least 5cm surrounding them as they spread out a lot while cooking. You might need to bake them in batches.

Bake for 12–15 minutes until golden or 5 minutes more for very crisp. Allow the cookies to cool on the baking sheet for 5 minutes before transferring to a wire rack to cool completely.

Cookies are great fun to experiment with. Just about anything goes. My favourites include strawberry and white chocolate, and gooseberry and dark chocolate.

MAKES ABOUT 30

225g unsalted butter, softened
185g granulated white sugar
220g light brown sugar
250g plain flour, sifted
½ tsp bicarbonate of soda, sifted
pinch of salt
250g rolled oats (I tend to use quite big plump organic ones)
8 passionfruit, halved and flesh scooped out with a spoon
1 egg, beaten
200g white chocolate chips

Rhubarb and Rosewater Fairy Cakes

MAKES 12

125g rhubarb, chopped into
1cm pieces, washed and
drained (a few droplets of
water here will help)
1 tbsp light brown sugar
125g unsalted butter, softened
125g caster sugar
125g self-raising flour, sifted
1 tsp baking powder, sifted
2 large eggs
1 vanilla pod, split open
lengthways

FOR THE ROSEWATER ICING

30g unsalted butter, softened
50g cream cheese
60g icing sugar, sifted
8 tsp rosewater

FOR THE RHUBARB BUTTERCREAM

50g rhubarb (choose the deepest
pink pieces), thinly sliced
1 tbsp caster sugar
25g butter
4 tsp icing sugar

These moist little fruity cakes with satiny icing are the kind of treats I imagine, and hope, I will make one day with my own children. Little fingers resembling mine curled round a wooden spoon. How useful to have some little assistants to help with the workload!

Rhubarb and rosewater go beautifully together – fruit and floral paired, just as in nature. I am using forced rhubarb, which is grown in dark, clandestine sheds and harvested by eerie candlelight. The Persians were the first to use rosewater as food. It was also used for bathing, and as a cure for depression in the Middle Ages and the Renaissance. Shakespeare described the sails of Cleopatra's ship as scented with it: 'the very winds were lovesick'. I find it surprisingly adaptable. As well as whipping it into cream for strawberries, I also stir it into a little cream, ground almonds and black pepper for a mughlai marinade for chicken, harking back to those Persians who first discovered its allure.

Preheat the oven to 190°C/Fan 170°C/Gas 5, and line a 12-bun muffin tin with cases.

Place the rhubarb in a pan with the sugar. Cover and cook over a very low heat for 4 minutes. Set aside.

Cut the butter into small pieces and place in a large mixing bowl. Add the sugar, flour, baking powder and eggs, and the seeds scraped out of the vanilla pod. Beat until smooth and evenly mixed. I do this by hand, and it works well.

Chop the rhubarb into small dice and add to the mixture, gently incorporating. Divide the mixture between the cases and bake for 18–20 minutes until golden and springy when touched. Cool slightly, then transfer to a wire rack to cool completely.

To make the rosewater icing, beat the butter and cream cheese in a bowl using an electric mixer, or in a food processor, then gradually add the icing sugar and beat again. Finally add the rosewater and beat till smooth. Spread a thinnish layer over the cooled cakes. Leave to set while making the buttercream.

Place the rhubarb in a pan with the caster sugar and cook, covered, on a very low heat for 4–5 minutes until very soft. Leave to cool completely. Using a spoon, beat this with the butter and icing sugar until pink and smooth. Use a piping bag to pipe little rosettes on the centre of each cake.

Perhaps try berry fruits as flavourings, or mango. I have rhubarb left over after making this, which I often add to rice. I like rice with the bumble-bee colours of black olives and yellow cherry tomatoes, coriander and stock, adding tiny flakes of rhubarb at the end for a touch of tartness.

WITH ITS PRINCELY CROWN and leathery skin, what treasure the pomegranate conceals. Its garnet seeds with their sweet yet tart juice are high reward for those who battle through the tough outer peel and clinging pith.

The pomegranate has fascinated people for centuries. The Ancient Egyptians referred to it as the 'first among fruits'. The Phoenicians spread it around the Mediterranean, and the Moors brought it to Spain around 800AD, where the city of Granada was named after it. Inspired by the way pomegranate seeds scatter, the French named their hand-tossed explosive, the grenade, after the fruit. In Britain, it was King Henry VIII who first planted it.

In Jewish custom, it is believed that the pomegranate has 613 seeds, representing the 613 commandments of the Torah. Some believe that it was the pomegranate that was the forbidden fruit of the tree of life in the biblical garden of Eden, and the fruit features in many religious paintings. In the Quran, it is said that it is a fruit of paradise, one of the good things that God creates. The Prophet Mohammed encourages followers to eat them to deflect envy and hatred from others. All the seeds must be eaten, because it is not known which have come from paradise.

Chilli and Pomegranate Chocolate Brownies

I first made these when I was woken, shivering, at 5am by a nightmare. Spooked and unable to drift back to sleep, I found myself in the sanctuary of my kitchen, concocting a double endorphin hit from the chocolate and chilli to soothe myself. I had some pomegranate kernels in the fridge from lunch, so, in my half-sleep, their fuchsia crunchiness went in too. They turned out incredibly well, distracting me completely from the ghoulish spectres, and I now make them all the time, at slightly more sensible times of the day.

MAKES 9 OR 18 SMALL

110g unsalted butter
150g dark chocolate
170g caster sugar
2 eggs, beaten
55g plain flour
30g cocoa powder
½ tsp baking powder
240g pomegranate kernels
½ tsp chilli powder

Preheat the oven to 180°C/Fan 160°C/Gas 4. Line an 18cm square tin with baking parchment.

Melt the butter and chocolate over a low heat. Stir in the sugar, then remove from the heat and cool to room temperature. Stir in the eggs. Sift the flour, cocoa and baking powder together and then fold into the chocolate. Stir in the pomegranate and chilli powder.

Spread the mixture out evenly in the tin and bake for 30 minutes. Allow to cool and then cut into squares.

Maybe add cherries instead, or some pistachio nuts. Increase or decrease the chilli as you see fit.

Sweet Potato Cinnamon Fritti with Sour Cherry Syrup and Clove Maple Ice Cream

SERVES 6 (MAKES 20–22 FRITTI)

FOR THE CLOVE MAPLE ICE CREAM
500ml vanilla ice cream,
    softened (see page 208)
1/4 tsp ground cloves
2 tbsp maple syrup

FOR THE SOUR CHERRY SYRUP
125g granulated sugar
250ml water
40g sweetened dried sour
    cherries

FOR THE FRITTI
4 sweet potatoes
75g plain flour, sifted
4 tbsp sugar
2 tsp baking powder, sifted
1 tsp ground cinnamon
1/2 tsp salt
2 large eggs, beaten
vegetable oil, for deep-frying
icing sugar, for dusting

This warming dessert with hints of New England flavours is one I like to make on a late autumn afternoon, when the leaves are defiantly ablaze in one last grand gesture and just before the sky dips into twilight. It's a lovely bowl to huddle up with on the sofa. Ground clove is a very strong flavour to add to the ice cream, so you only need a tiny amount. Which is lucky, considering it was once worth more than its weight in gold. Cloves are originally from the Malacca Islands, now part of Indonesia, where the trees were planted to celebrate the birth of a baby, the fate of the child believed to be intertwined with that of the tree.

First boil the sweet potatoes for the fritti, whole in their skins, for about 20–25 minutes until soft. Cool, peel and mash. You should have about 400g of cooked flesh. Set aside.

Mix the softened ice cream with the ground cloves and maple syrup. Place in a container and refreeze until firm.

For the syrup, heat the sugar and water in a pan over a low heat, stirring occasionally to help the sugar dissolve. When the sugar has dissolved, turn up the heat and bring to the boil. Add the cherries and boil for 5 minutes. Switch off the heat and set aside.

For the fritti, stir the flour, sugar, baking powder, cinnamon and salt together in a bowl. In another large bowl, whisk the mashed sweet potato into the eggs. Add the flour mixture into this and stir until just combined.

Deep-fry the fritti by dropping dessertspoonfuls into the hot oil in a deep pan in batches. (The oil is hot enough when a bit of batter, dropped in for testing, rises to the surface.) Fry for about 4 minutes until golden, then drain on kitchen paper.

Dust with icing sugar and serve with the clove maple ice cream and the sour cherry syrup.

Try making with pumpkin instead, and maybe a cranberry syrup. Or a peanut butter ice cream.

Hibiscus Berry Soup with Lemongrass Boudoir Biscuits

Based on a Hungarian cherry soup, my recipe uses an assortment of berries (you could use just one kind if you prefer) and hibiscus. With its slightly astringent flavour, hibiscus contrasts well with the sweetness of the fruit. I used Hibi hibiscus juice, which is available in little bottles.

   Although I enjoyed the soup both hot and cold, it felt like it was missing something, something to dunk into it and soak up all the juices. I thought of the sponges in trifles and so looked into this a little. I cannot deny that the enticing name 'boudoir biscuits' did influence my decision somewhat. The recipe I adapted was from Le Cordon Bleu and I found them a delight to make. However, they did say on their recipe that I needed to tap away the sugar from the baking paper after dusting the biscuits and before they go in the oven. This I found virtually impossible to do as there seemed to be no way to get it off without disturbing the batter. So I just left it on. I thought it might burn and be a disaster, but nothing happened at all, so I have left this instruction out.

   I also added some very fine flakes of lemongrass to the boudoir biscuits, to complement the berries. I could have used lemon but wanted something a bit more exotic to go with the hibiscus. This powerfully scented stalk is what I imagine the love child of lemon and ginger to taste like. When I sat eating this, the world seemed so very small, so many ingredients and influences from all over the world sitting in my little bowl.

Preheat the oven to 180°C/Fan 160°C/Gas 4. Grease 2 baking trays with butter and line with baking parchment.

   Using an electric mixer, beat the egg whites until they form stiff peaks. Gradually beat in the sugar until stiff peaks form again and the egg whites are glossy and smooth. Lightly beat the egg yolks and then fold into the meringued egg whites with a wooden spoon, along with the lemongrass. Sift the cake flour over this and then fold in gently.

   Pour the mixture into an icing or pastry bag and, using a large plain tip, pipe lengths of 12.5cm and 2cm thick on to the baking parchment, leaving a few centimetres surrounding each one. Sift icing sugar over the top, wait 5 minutes, then dust again with sifted icing sugar.

   Bake in the oven for 10 minutes, then turn the baking tray round so they colour evenly and bake for a further 5 minutes. Remove from the baking tray with a spatula while still hot and allow to cool on a wire rack.

FOR THE LEMONGRASS BOUDOIR BISCUITS

MAKES ABOUT 16

3 eggs, separated
6 tbsp white granulated sugar
4 tbsp very finely chopped
    lemongrass, like small flakes
100g cake flour, made by
    mixing 75g plain flour
    and 25g cornflour
icing sugar, for dusting

250g caster sugar
750ml Hibi hibiscus juice
240ml crème fraîche
900g mixed berries
    (strawberries, blueberries,
    blackberries, raspberries, etc)
chopped mint leaves, to garnish

Place the caster sugar in a large pan with the hibiscus juice, and stir over a low heat to dissolve. When dissolved, turn up the heat and boil for 5 minutes. Then turn down to very low and allow it to settle. Add the crème fraîche, turn up the heat slightly and simmer gently for 5 minutes, stirring occasionally. (You can cook the soup up to this point in advance and reheat it just before serving.)

Serve the soup warm but not hot. Stir in the berries and garnish with chopped mint. Serve with the biscuits to dunk in.

Use red grape juice if you prefer. Or you could do a light version with white grape juice and white currants with vanilla boudoir biscuits. Try cold sweet soups served in little cups, such as strawberry whizzed with a little sherry, served with basil leaf, black pepper and a little lemon oil.

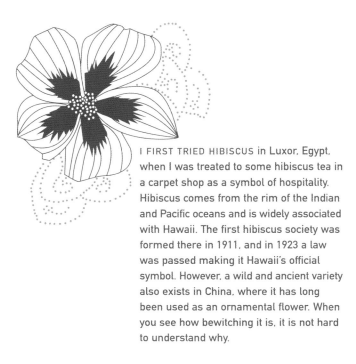

I FIRST TRIED HIBISCUS in Luxor, Egypt, when I was treated to some hibiscus tea in a carpet shop as a symbol of hospitality. Hibiscus comes from the rim of the Indian and Pacific oceans and is widely associated with Hawaii. The first hibiscus society was formed there in 1911, and in 1923 a law was passed making it Hawaii's official symbol. However, a wild and ancient variety also exists in China, where it has long been used as an ornamental flower. When you see how bewitching it is, it is not hard to understand why.

Sesame and Coconut Cookies with Lemon Thyme Dipping Sauce

MAKES ABOUT 34 SMALL COOKIES

This was a fluke recipe in that, when I made it, I had no idea what the cookies were going to turn out like. I just wanted to use up ingredients that were taking up space, so I bunged everything together in a bowl, stirred it all and put the mix in the oven. I was surprised it was edible, let alone so tasty.

The sesame seeds and coconut had been bought for a religious blessing, a Havan, which had recently taken place in my home. I had been burgled some weeks beforehand, and my best friend Jigna, a Hindu, was adamant I should have a ceremony to purify the house of any ill effects of the evil eye she thought was responsible.

It was fascinating to learn of the mystical powers the fruits, nuts and seeds are believed to have. Doing as I was told, I dropped spoonfuls of ghee and spices into the small fire that was lit, the pungent smell weaving its way through all the rooms while prayers were said for curses to be broken and old ghosts to leave. To my surprise, a red thread was tied round a coconut and my wrist, with a prayer from the priest to bring forth my future husband. Two ceremonies for the price of one, I thought.

115g unsalted butter

110g light brown sugar

2 large eggs, beaten

70g sesame seeds, toasted

100g desiccated unsweetened
   coconut

125g plain flour, sifted

1 tsp baking powder, sifted

Preheat the oven to 190°C/Fan 170°C/Gas 5. Line a baking tray with baking parchment.

Melt the butter and allow it to cool a bit. In a large mixing bowl, combine all the ingredients together and mix well. Make tablespoon-sized balls, flattening each slightly and placing on the baking sheet with a few centimetres between them. Bake for 10 minutes or until golden brown. Cool for 1–2 minutes before eating warm with the hot lemon sauce, or allow to cool fully on wire racks.

FOR THE LEMON THYME DIPPING
SAUCE

175ml double cream

1 tbsp lemon curd

3 sprigs lemon thyme

Place all the ingredients in a pan and heat through, gently simmering for a few minutes, then allow to cool slightly before serving with the cookies.

Try with a different sauce, such as a chocolate one.

Chargrilled Pineapple with Salted Caramel

SERVES 4

butter, for griddling the
   pineapple
pineapple wedges for
   4–6 people
150 golden caster sugar
125ml double cream
80g salted butter
1 tsp coarse sea salt

I like my salted caramel discernibly salty with the juicy pineapple. Try it like this, just to see what your taste buds make of it, then you can always reduce the salt on another occasion if you prefer. The caramel will begin to harden upon cooling, so make sure you serve it just after it is made, and soak the pan well in hot water straight away for easy cleaning.

Melt a bit of butter in a griddle pan and cook the pineapple until slightly charred on each side. Set aside and keep warm.

Place the golden caster sugar in a heavy-based saucepan without any water and set over a low heat, without stirring, until the sugar caramelises and turns amber. Add the cream – careful as it may splutter, so stand back – and stir in the butter. Simmer for a couple of minutes, switch off the heat and then stir in the sea salt before serving with the pineapple.

Try griddling other fruits, such as nectarines, peaches, sharon fruits, mango. Try the salted caramel sauce over ice cream or bananas

WITH

Here are some bready recipes that work well with steaming mugs of coffee, soothing cups of tea or on the table alongside your main dishes. The slightly charred Leek Flatbreads are just as good with a tall glass of dense, Middle Eastern–style inky coffee in the morning as torn and eaten with the Garam Masala Chicken and Basil Couscous at dinnertime. There are also some ideas here for breakfast, such as the Pancakes with Canteloupe, Maple and Bacon, although they are just as delicious at teatime too. The Baked Eggs are particularly good on weekend evenings with hot buttered soldiers or brunch with asparagus spears to dip into the creamy concoction as they are for breakfast.

And of course, there's something to sip alongside the food in the book. Whether you are after a festive tipple like the Cherry, Amaretto and Champagne Sparkler, something light to provide a cooling foil for spicy food like the Cucumber Water or a cup of something warming for gloved fingers to clutch outdoors in the winter months like the Red Apple Hot Ginger Fizz, there's a selection of drinks to help wash down the dishes you create.

BREAD AND BREAKFAST

Bruschetta with Soft Cheese, Tomato and Honey
Pancakes with Cantaloupe, Maple and Bacon
Mustard, Green Olive and Cheddar Scones
Leek Flatbreads with Horseradish Butter
Mooli, Lemon and Feta Muffins
Baked Eggs with Anchovy, Capers and Olives
Fennel, Salami and Pistachio Loaf
Garlic Yogurt Potato Cakes with Smoked Salmon

TO WASH DOWN

Cherry, Amaretto and Champagne Sparkler
Cucumber Water
Apricot Honey Iced Green Tea
Avocado and Cumin Milkshake Shorts
Raspberry Limeade
Red Apple Hot Ginger Fizz
Saffron Blood Orangeade

Bruschetta with Soft Cheese, Tomato and Honey

SERVES 2

4 bruschetta or thin slices of
  ciabatta
olive oil
4 tbsp cream cheese
1 tsp honey
2 tomatoes, thinly sliced

My friend Ginnie told me of eating a wedge of Parmesan in Italy drizzled with honey, which she thought was rather splendid. Thus, I thought I'd try a little thread of honey over some cream cheese, not as salty as Parmesan, but hopefully still enough to have a similar effect. I liked it very much, adding a few wafer-thin slices of ripe tomatoes and black pepper.

Take 4 thin slices of ciabatta bread, brush with olive oil and griddle in a pan or grill till crisp and browned, then drizzle with a little more. Spread a tablespoon of cream cheese on each slice. Drizzle over a little honey. Add a couple of slices of tomato and grind some black pepper over. Bruschetta comes from the Italian word meaning to 'burn slightly', *bruscare*.

Certainly try with Parmesan and other cheeses, such as Quark.

THE BOTANICAL NAME FOR THE TOMATO, *Lycopersicon esculentum*, means 'wolfpeach' because it was thought of as a round, succulent fruit deceptively resembling a peach, but one that was poisonous. A member of the deadly nightshade family, tomatoes were thought to be poisonous when the conquistadores discovered them growing in South and Central America. When Cortés brought the seeds back to Europe in 1519, they were grown for ornamental purposes, the yellow variety most likely the first. The French, however, looked upon the fruit more favourably over time, and called them *pommes d'amour*, or 'love apples'.

Pancakes with Cantaloupe, Maple and Bacon

SERVES 4

1 tbsp golden syrup

15g butter

150ml milk, plus 1 tbsp

175g plain flour

1 tsp cream of tartar

2 tsp baking powder

25g caster sugar

pinch of salt

1 egg, beaten

to serve: thin slices of
    cantaloupe melon, rashers
    of crisply grilled streaky
    bacon and maple syrup

optional extras: fresh coriander
    leaves, crushed chillies in oil

This has long been one of my favourite summer breakfasts. I love the ripe orange flesh of the melon, dripping with honeyed juices, on the golden pancakes with salty strips of crisped streaky bacon and a dribble of mahogany maple syrup. I like to add a few teardrops of oily crushed chilli and some freshly ripped coriander leaf too.

Place the syrup, butter and the tablespoon of milk in a small pan, heating gently until the ingredients are melted, then leave to cool.

Sift the dry ingredients together in a mixing bowl, then make a dip in the centre. Add the egg, melted ingredients and half the milk, then combine well into a batter. Stir in the remaining milk, beat for a couple of minutes until the batter has a thick consistency, then let stand for 15 minutes.

Lightly grease a heavy-based frying pan and warm it over a medium heat. Drop tablespoons of the batter on to the pan and cook until bubbles rise
to the surface and burst. Turn the pancakes over with a palette knife and continue cooking until golden brown, then keep warm while making the rest.

Layer the pancakes with thin slices of cantaloupe melon, rashers of crisply grilled streaky bacon, maple syrup, chopped fresh coriander leaves and a little crushed chilli.

You could try this with honeydew melon, or even a few berries instead. I also make a cantaloupe, bacon and feta salad, adding torn fresh mint leaves, chilli, cumin and extra virgin olive oil.

Mustard, Green Olive and Cheddar Scones

For breakfast, I like eating these split in half horizontally, topped with a slice of halloumi that has been dusted in seasoned flour and fried in butter till golden, and finally a poached egg, leaking its golden centre over everything and seeping into the scones. But they are also good cut and toasted and spread just with a little butter.

I think the mustard really adds flavour here. I like all varieties, from English to dark French, but wholegrain works particularly well.

Preheat the oven to 200°C/Fan 180°C/Gas 6.

Sift the flour, baking powder and salt together in a bowl. Add the cheese, olives and mustard, and mix well with a spoon.

Mix the cream and milk together in a jug, then beat in the large egg. Slowly pour the egg mixture into the dry ingredients in the bowl and fold in, combining into a soft, loose dough. It should not be sticky, so add a little more flour if needed.

Gently lift the dough out and shape with your hands on a floured surface into a round about 2.5cm thick. Cut into 8 wedge-like triangles, like a pizza. If your knife gets sticky cutting through, coat the blade with a bit of flour each time you do so. Place on a greased baking tray, brush the tops and sides well with egg wash and bake at top of the oven for around 25 minutes or until golden brown.

Serve split in half horizontally.

You could use different types of mustard, black or kalamata olives, and perhaps another type of cheese. Why not blue cheese scones? Or even Wensleydale and a bit of cranberry relish.

MAKES 8 SCONE WEDGES

420g plain flour, plus extra for dusting
20g baking powder
1 tsp salt
125g Cheddar, grated
85g olives, chopped
5 tbsp wholegrain mustard
125ml double cream
125ml milk, plus a couple of tablespoons extra for the egg wash
1 large egg, plus an extra egg for the egg wash mixed with milk

Leek Flatbreads with Horseradish Butter

SERVES 2–4

2 tbsp salted butter, softened

1/2 tsp fresh horseradish

2 tbsp mild olive oil, plus 1 tsp for frying

1 leek, halved lengthways and thinly sliced

255g plain flour, sifted

These are a bit of a cross between Indian parathe and Middle Eastern flatbreads. You could eat them alongside a meal with yoghurt and Lebanese pickles. I love them crispy and almost burnt, on Sunday mornings with a tableful of newspapers and a pot of some very strong black coffee.

Mix the butter and horseradish together, adding some black pepper and a bit of sea salt if you wish, then cover with cling film and refrigerate while you cook the breads.

Heat the teaspoon of olive oil in a frying pan and fry the leek on a high heat for 3 minutes with a good grind of pepper, then set aside to cool.

In a bowl, mix the flour, mild olive oil and leek together with a few pinches of salt, using a metal spoon and pressing out any lumps. Add 125ml hot water, binding everything together, then work into a dough, kneading for a few minutes until soft and elastic – it should not be sticky but nice and smooth. Place in a bowl, cover with cling film or a damp tea towel and leave for about 20 minutes at room temperature.

Divide and shape into 4 balls and, using a little flour to prevent sticking, roll out to a couple of millimetres thick. Preheat a non-stick frying pan till hot.

Dry-fry one at a time over a medium heat (not too hot or you'll blister the outsides but the insides won't be cooked) for about 2 minutes on either side until crispy, then spread with the horseradish butter.

Try using spring onions instead and a wasabi butter. Or maybe a bit of mustard in the butter and some red onions in the flatbreads.

Mooli, Lemon and Feta Muffins

MAKES 12 MUFFINS

150g wholemeal self-raising
flour
200g white self-raising flour
½ tsp bicarbonate of soda
½ tsp baking powder
1 tsp salt
200g grated mooli flesh,
squeezed of excess water
200g feta, crumbled
4 preserved lemons, pips
removed, finely chopped
3 tbsp finely chopped chives
300ml milk, soured with 1 tsp
fresh lemon juice
2 eggs
100ml olive oil

The mooli in this does not impart a flavour as such but rather a
moistness, and thus you can use another vegetable that will have
the same effect instead, such as courgette, pumpkin or carrot. I
like the slight nuttiness the wholemeal flour lends, grounding the
sharper flavours of the preserved lemons and feta, plus a hit of allium
from the chives.

Preheat the oven to 200°C/Fan 180°C/Gas 6, and line a 12-bun muffin
tin with cases.

Sift the wholemeal flour (when only bran is left in the sieve, chuck
that into the bowl too), white flour, bicarbonate of soda, baking powder,
salt and a good grind of pepper into a mixing bowl. Add the mooli, feta,
preserved lemon and chives and mix well.

Whisk the milk, eggs and oil together and stir into the dry ingredients
until just combined. Divide between the muffin cases and bake for
around 25 minutes or until golden and springy.

Try making with different vegetables and maybe swap the lemons for
some olives or capers. Try with goat's cheese too.

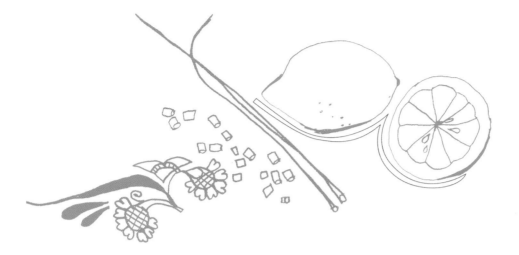

Baked Eggs with Anchovy, Capers and Olives

These are among my favourite things, especially good on Sunday evenings. I think of them almost as a savoury crème brûlée in terms of the luxurious texture and the cayenne-dusted tops, which I like a little crispy. I love dipping into the salty creaminess with wholemeal toasted soldiers, shimmering with a little butter. I also often have them cold the next day, tucking straight into the glass ramekins with nothing but a little spoon.

Preheat the oven to 190°C/Fan 170°C/Gas 5. Lightly grease 4 ramekins with butter.

Put 2 tablespoons of the puttanesca mixture in the bottom of each ramekin. Sprinkle over some chopped parsley. Pour a tablespoon of cream in each and then crack an egg over the top. Pour another tablespoon of cream over the egg. Sprinkle with some Parmesan and finally some cayenne pepper.

Place the ramekins in a roasting tin and pour boiling water in to come half-way up the sides of the dishes to create a bain-marie. Bake for 20 minutes.

You could make these with chopped pimento-stuffed olives, or just olives or capers or anchovies. You might also like them with pieces of roasted pepper, or pancetta, or wild mushrooms.

SERVES 4

180g jar puttanesca mix, drained (drained weight 110g) or a third each of chopped anchovy, sliced black olives and capers
chopped parsley
120ml double cream
4 eggs
grated Parmesan
cayenne pepper

Fennel, Salami and Pistachio Loaf

I thought I would try tinkering with the useful packet mixes you can get now, although, of course, you could use these ingredients in a loaf made from scratch. I wanted a moist loaf studded with unique flavours and beautiful colours, to eat simply on its own, warm from the oven. I like buttery green nibs of pistachio nuts in savoury dishes as well as sweet desserts. The first archaeological findings of them are from the Paleozoic period, 6760 BC, around where Jordan is today. They have long been considered the foodstuff of the rich and the chosen. Apparently they were a favourite of the Queen of Sheba.

Preheat the oven to 230°C/Fan 210°C/Gas 8.

Heat a non-stick frying pan and add the fennel. Cook for 3 minutes with a pinch of salt, just to colour a little.

Place the bread mix in a bowl, stir in the fennel, salami and pistachios, then gradually add 300ml warm water. Mix together for 5 minutes to combine in a soft dough.

Lift out and place on a floured surface for 5 minutes. Knead for 2 minutes, then let it stand for 5 minutes again. Mould the dough into an oval loaf shape and place on a greased baking tray, cover with a damp tea towel and leave to rise in a warm place for 30–40 minutes, until doubled in size.

Dust with flour and bake in the middle of the oven for 25 minutes or until golden brown.

Breads are a great way to try flavours, I love anchovy fougasse, for example. Play around with two or three flavours, and bake in a loaf tin if you prefer.

MAKES 1 LOAF

half a bulb of fennel, plus some fronds, finely chopped

500g pack of mixed-grain speciality bread mix, or another variety you prefer

15 slices of salami (I like the black pepper variety), chopped into small squares

25g pistachios, smashed with a pestle in a mortar or pulsed in a food processor until broken into small nibs

Garlic Yoghurt Potato Cakes with Smoked Salmon

MAKES 16

2 large potatoes, scrubbed

2 tsp mild olive oil

2 garlic cloves, crushed

2 tbsp finely chopped dill

mild olive oil, for frying

8 tbsp natural yoghurt (I prefer
   live as it has a tangy taste)

enough smoked salmon for 4
   people

1 lemon

a few capers

I adore these, but you have to be careful with them when cooking so as not to burn them, and also not to break them when you flip them over because they are very soft when first in the pan. In fact, it is best not to touch or disturb them at all for the first couple of minutes so that they can crisp up on the underside. Then slide the fish slice under to fully support the patty and quickly flip over in one swift movement, so they don't tear.

Place the potatoes, skins still on, in a large pan of cold water. Bring to the boil and boil for about 20 minutes until soft. Remove the skins and mash the flesh in a bowl.

Heat the olive oil in a pan over a low heat and fry the garlic very lightly and quickly for only a few seconds, just to colour slightly. Add to the potato with the dill and season with salt. Stir in the yoghurt, gradually, to create a smooth mixture.

Heat a centimetre of oil in a large frying pan. Take ping-pong-ball-size amounts of the mixture, roll into balls, then gently flatten as thin as you can without it breaking. You will need to wet your hands slightly in between rolling balls to stop the mixture sticking to your skin and the patties breaking.

Fry in batches of about 4 at a time. Once added to the oil, do not move or touch for 2 minutes or they will break. Then use a fish slice and carefully and quickly flip over. Cook for another $1\frac{1}{2}$–2 minutes until cooked. Drain on kitchen paper and keep warm.

Top with smoked salmon, a good squeeze of lemon juice and a couple of capers.

You could make croquettes with the potato mixture, rolling and coating with egg wash and breadcrumbs and then baking till crisp.

Cherry, Amaretto and Champagne Sparkler

I serve this to guests upon their arrival at my home at Christmas. The seasonal colours are sensational, especially with a few fresh cranberries adorning the glass like the gleaming baubles on a festive tree. You could use prosecco, cava, Alsace crémant, or a non-alcoholic sparkling drink such as Shloer or Amé instead of Champagne, if you like.

SERVES 6

400g can of morello cherries (you won't use them all)
1 bottle of Champagne
Amaretto syrup (for coffees)

Whiz up some morello cherries to create a purée and spoon a little in the bottom of Champagne flutes. Top up with chilled Champagne and lace with a drizzle of Amaretto syrup.

Try puréeing other fruits and topping with a sparkling drink, or, in an unusual pairing of flavours, try lacing a simple glass of Champagne with a coffee-flavoured syrup, adding a few coffee beans in the bottom, or drizzle in some honey.

Cucumber Water

It was the excellent food and wine writer, Fiona Beckett, who gave me the idea for this drink. As I was pretty sceptical of matching wine with Indian food, I had been invited to try a whole range of wines with Fiona for a piece we put together for *Decanter* magazine. I cooked a range of dishes and, for a couple of days, my home was invaded by box upon box of assorted wines. Fiona arrived and we ate and tasted, trying to find a good match.

Out of all of them, there was only one that I was seriously impressed with and thought supported the flavours of Indian food, complementing rather than competing with them. That was the Alsace pinot gris.

However, as we were sat at the table, I also made Fiona a quick lassi, stirring spoonfuls of yoghurt into cold water and ice, which she highly enjoyed with the food. Talking of this, and thinking of the flavours of a cucumber raita, we thought a cool cucumber drink might also be suitably refreshing: thus inspiring this simple drink.

SERVES 2–4

1 cucumber
ice
Champagne or prosecco (optional)

Peel, halve and deseed a cucumber, purée it in a blender, then strain to serve either on its own with ice or half and half with water or chilled Champagne or prosecco and a curl of cucumber for a refreshing cocktail.

Try scenting Champagne with lemongrass by infusing it with freshly cut flakes for an hour before straining it into glasses. You could even serve it with a few strips of the stalk in the glass.

Apricot Honey Iced Green Tea

SERVES 8

1kg fresh apricots, peeled and
chopped
150g granulated sugar
a few pinches of bicarbonate of
soda
2 green tea bags
4 tbsp runny honey

This is a fruity alternative to regular refreshing black iced tea. It is thought that the drinking of tea began in Burma and China. There is a legend that it was discovered by the Chinese emperor Shen Nung in 2737 BC when some dried tea leaves from a bush fell into his cup of hot water. Tea-drinking spread around south Asia before the Europeans began trading it from China in the seventeenth century. There was certainly a taste for it. By the early nineteenth century, at the height of the East India Company, Britain was drinking nine million cups of tea a year

Purée the apricot in a blender with the sugar and bicarbonate of soda. Bring 1 litre of water to the boil. After 5 minutes (so that the water doesn't scald the tea), pour over the green tea bags in a jug and steep for 4 minutes. Remove the tea bags, add the apricot purée and honey, stir and allow to cool. Once cool, strain through muslin or kitchen paper and top with 600ml cold water. Serve over ice.

Try this with weak black tea if you like. Perhaps also try making a chilled version with black tea and fresh blackcurrants with a hint of lime zest.

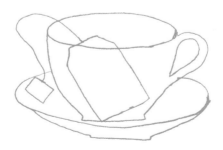

Avocado and Cumin Milkshake Shorts

SERVES 4 AS SMALL SERVINGS

120ml milk

120ml buttermilk

1 avocado, chopped into small
  pieces

1/2 tsp ground cumin

finely chopped mint

1 lime, quartered

I love avocado milkshakes short and frothy with lots of ice and a bit of earthy cumin, just as we add to Indian lassi. As avocado is so creamy, I like to cut through it a bit with tangy buttermilk and lime.

Whizz the milk, buttermilk, avocado and cumin together in a blender and serve over ice, topped with a little mint and with lime juice squeezed over.

You could add a little jalapeño chilli to this for a bit of heat.

Raspberry Limeade

This is very refreshing and great for summer picnics and parties, with just enough sweet fruit to balance the sharpness of the lime. The colours of this fizzing thirst quencher are also beautiful in a tall jug, with plenty of ice. It is just the thing to enjoy outdoors at an August gathering, effervescent glasses clinking.

Blend the raspberries with the lime juice and sugar, then top up with the sparkling water. Strain, stir in the zest and chill. Serve with ice.

Try other berry fruits, or gooseberries with a couple of vanilla pods in the jug.

SERVES 4
1 kg raspberries
the juice of 4 limes
100g granulated sugar
700ml sparkling water
the zest of 2 limes

Red Apple Hot Ginger Fizz

SERVES 6

6 red apples, skin on, chopped
   into small chunks
2 sticks of cinnamon
20g light brown sugar
1.5 litre bottle of ginger ale
a handful of chopped mint
   leaves

This recipe was inspired by the toffee-like taste of the rich red apple juice I have had in Canada. These hot little cups of fruity warmth, spiced with a couple of cinnamon quills, are easy to make and perfect clutched in cold hands while you're having a bonfire or watching fireworks explode across the sky. You might also like to add a few slices of fresh ginger to the pan.

Whizz 4 apples' worth of chunks in a food processor, transfer to a large pan, add the the cinnamon, sugar and ginger ale and heat through gently for about 5 minutes. Take off the heat and allow to infuse for another 5 minutes. Strain and pour into cups over some of the remaining chunks of apple, and add the chopped mint.

For a more vigorous flavour, try ginger beer instead of ginger ale.

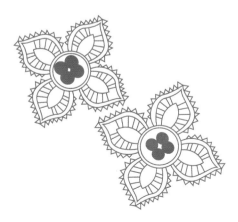

Saffron Blood Orangeade

I like the slight muskiness the saffron brings to this drink, which I serve in Moroccan cups. But the orange has not always been the sweet fruit we have come to love. The original incarnation was a sour one that grew wild in China, and was also thought to have roots in Burma and the Assam region of India. These oriental treasures remained in the East for a long time before capturing the hearts of the Romans. In fact, they are even called 'Chinese apple' in some languages. The word 'orange' comes from the ancient Sanskrit for orange tree: *naranja*. The Moors planted them across Africa in the first century AD, bringing them to Spain in the eight or ninth century. The Saracens took them to Sicily, planting them there too. Christopher Columbus took them across the pond. They reached the west coast when the Spanish brought them to Florida in 1565 and so, eventually, the orange had travelled right round the globe.

SERVES 6

75g caster sugar
1 tbsp saffron strands steeped in
   2 tbsp hot water
juice of 6 blood oranges
zest of 3 blood oranges
soda water, to taste

Place the sugar in a pan with 600ml water. Bring to the boil, dissolving the sugar, and then simmer for 5 minutes. Stir in the saffron water and the orange juice and zest, and allow to cool.

Strain, then top up with soda water.

Perhaps try an orange and lemon version. Or a mixed citrus one with lemon, lime, orange and grapefruit.

GOLDEN SAFFRON is the stigma of the crocus flower. Originally from the Mediterranean region, the flower was probably spread by Phoenician sailors all over the Middle East and Europe. The name comes from the Arabic *zafaran*, meaning 'yellow'. It is said that the armies of Alexander the Great were so seduced by Persian pilaffs, whose scent they found intoxicating, that they would refuse to do battle until they had slept off its dizzying effects.

USEFUL STUFF

BASIC RECIPES

Sometimes it just takes a few twists here and there to create something with unique flavours, and the best way to do this is to try the ingredient combinations in a very basic, neutral recipe. Here are some to get you started. Add your own flavours as you wish.

MARINADES

Mix flavorings together with a sweetener such as honey, sugar or maple syrup and a souring agent such as lemon, lime or balsamic and use to marinade meats. Alternatively, whizz up your chosen flavourings with a few spoonfuls of natural yoghurt.

DIPS

For some simple base dips that you can customize, use mild Welsh goat's cheese with some Greek yoghurt to loosen or whizz canned chickpeas, broadbeans, cannelini or butterbeans with a little yoghurt, olive oil and tahini.

For fresh, salsa dips, place some chopped onion, red onion or spring onion in a blender with some chopped tomatoes and other ingredients, herbs and flavourings of your choice and pulse until finely chopped and well mixed.

TRAY-GRILLED POTATOES

This is another dish to which you can add ingredients to customise each time. Chop any potatoes, skin left on, into bite-size pieces, rinse and then boil until cooked all the way through. Turn onto an oiled baking tray and scatter with semolina, add other ingredients and flavourings to the tray, drizzle over some more olive oil and place under a very hot grill until golden.

RICE PILAFF

I probably make this more than anything else as it is extremely quick, easy, healthy, versatile, and it's an all-in-one-pan complete meal, so there's virtually no washing up. This recipe serves 2–4.

1 tbsp olive oil
½ onion (sliced)
1 cup of washed basmati rice

Heat the olive oil in a deep, large non-stick frying pan with a lid. I add some cumin seeds at this point, but you could just omit if you like and go straight onto adding some sliced onion. Use red, spring onion or shallots if you prefer. Stir well and when soft add any other ingredients (such as vegetables, nuts, bite size pieces of meat), flavourings, herbs, spices, crumbled stock (I would use ½ cube) you like into the pan before finally adding the rice, stirring and bringing to the boil. Then place the lid on and simmer on a very low heat for about 10–15 minutes, or until the water is all absorbed and the rice is cooked and fluffy. Serve with crème fraiche or yoghurt.

PLAIN WHITE SAUCE

20g butter
20g plain flour
290ml milk

Gently melt the butter, then remove the pan from the heat and briskly stir in the flour to make a smooth paste.

Place the pan back over a medium heat and stir continuously for about a minute, until the roux (the butter and flour mixture) begins to bubble. Remove the pan from the heat and allow to cool for about a minute.

Slowly add the milk a tablespoon at a time, continuously stirring to remove any lumps. When you have added half the milk and the mixture is smooth, add the remaining milk in one go and stir well to mix thoroughly.

Return the pan to the heat and cook over a medium heat, stirring all the time until boiling.

Boil the sauce for 2 mins to make sure the flour is cooked through. Add any flavourings you wish to add and allow to steep.

SYRUP

150g golden caster sugar
300ml water

Heat the sugar in a pan with 300ml water over a low heat, stirring occasionally to help the sugar dissolve. When dissolved, turn up the heat and boil for 5 minutes without stirring. Switch off the heat, allow to cool slightly for a minute before adding any flavours you like. Serve with fruits, drizzle over ice cream or add to drinks.

CARAMEL

This is a basic caramel which is very useful for desserts. You can stir in other flavours at the end such as orange blossom water or melt in some chocolate. Alternatively, leave plain and combine with the ingredients in your pudding.

225g granulated sugar
290ml water

Place the sugar in a heavy-based saucepan with half the water. Heat over a low heat until the sugar has dissolved, stirring occasionally to help it along. If the water starts to simmer before all the sugar has dissolved, turn the heat down further. It can take quite a few minutes for the sugar to dissolve. If sugar crystals begin to appear, or if at any point the sugar catches and begins to colour or burn along the sides of the pan, brush the sides of the pan down with a pastry brush dipped in cold water.

Once all the sugar has dissolved and you have a clear liquid, turn the heat to high and boil the mixture until it turns a deep amber colour. This takes about 10 minutes. Do not stir once it has begun to boil, but really watch the colour as it goes quickly from a lovely deep gold colour with a muskily sweet flavour to a burnt, bitter mess instead. Once it has reached the right colour, put an oven glove on, stand back, turn the heat off, and tip in the remaining water to stop it cooking. It may splutter, so be careful and swish the water round the pan to cool it quickly.

ICE CREAM

SERVES 4–6
290 ml whole milk
4 medium egg yolks
110g caster sugar
290ml whipping or double cream

Pour the milk into a saucepan and heat over a medium temperature until the milk begins to steam and little bubbles line around the edge of the pan.

Remove the pan from the heat and let it cool down slightly for about 10 mins.

Stir the sugar into the egg yolks in a bowl using a fork. Slowly stir the warm milk into this egg mixture and then pour this into a fresh clean pan.

Cook the mixture over a medium low heat, stirring it continuously with a wood spoon until the mixture thickens enough to coat the back of it. Do not overheat the mixture or it will curdle.

Immediately sieve the thickened mixture into a bowl, then place this bowl into a large container filled with ice cubes and leave to cool, stirring occasionally.

Stir the cream into this mixture and then pour into an ice cream maker to freeze. Add whatever flavours you fancy, such as vanilla pod seeds or fruits.

YOGHURT

Add savoury ingredients and flavours to yoghurt to serve as a dip, and fruits and sweet flavourings to make easy frozen yoghurt. To make FROZEN LASSI combine 125g natural low-fat yoghurt with ¼ tea-spoon garam masala, ¼ teaspoon ground cumin and ¼ teaspoon dried mint. Season with a little salt and pour into an ice-cube tray to freeze for several hours. I prefer to use trays with shapes, such as stars or long bars.

CUPCAKES

MAKES 12

125g unsalted butter, softened

125g caster sugar

125g self-raising flour, sifted

1 tsp baking powder

2 large eggs

A teaspoon of any spice or other flavouring
of your choice

125g diced fruit, nuts or chocolate chips – take
your pick

FOR THE ICING

150g unsalted butter, softened

250g icing sugar

1-2 tsp flavouring, such as vanilla extract,
flavoured syrup, fruit juice or espresso coffee

1-2 tsp hot water

Preheat the oven to 190°C/Fan 170°C/Gas 5.

Beat together the butter, sugar, flour, baking powder, eggs and any flavouring or spice in a large mixing bowl until it is evenly mixed and smooth.

Gently stir in any fruit or other ingredients you wish to add and then divide equally between cases in a muffin tray. Bake for about 20 minutes until golden.

Cool slightly in the tray and then place on a wire rack until fully cooled.

Beat the sugar and butter together till light and fluffy then add the flavourings and water as required until smooth and creamy, then spread or pipe on top of the cooled cakes.

KITCHEN ESSENTIALS

Of course the must-have ingredients in your kitchen will vary according to the types of foods you enjoy best and the flavours you wish to use. But just to give an example, here are the items I always have to hand, using them together and introducing new ingredients to create different flavour combinations.

In the storecupboards:
Rice – basmati and brown
Egg pasta
Noodles
Oats
Couscous

Self-raising flour
Plain flour
Wholemeal roti flour
Baking powder and bicarbonate of soda
Sugars – white, caster, brown, icing
Honey and maple syrup

Nuts
Olive oil and extra virgin olive oil
Stock cubes
Cumin seeds
Coriander seeds
Tumeric
Garam masala
Five spice
Soy sauce
Fish sauce
Tamarind
Balsamic vinegar
Ketchup
Mustard

Cooking salt and ground black pepper
Breadcrumbs

Onions
Tinned chickpeas and pulses
Coconut milk
Tinned fruit

In the fridge:
Bottled crushed red chilli
Plain yoghurt
Tomatoes
Butter
Lemons

In the freezer:
Packets of frozen herbs
Whole chillies
Grated ginger
Crushed garlic
Chopped lemongrass
Ready-rolled pastry sheets and cases
Frozen vegetables

YOUR UTENSIL KIT

Generally, you don't need many utensils to cook. I really don't use fancy equipment, nor anything particularly expensive. In addition to regular kitchen items such as tin-openers, graters and wooden spoons, these are the items I consider my essentials:

- A good quality large chef's knife that suits the size of your hand and your frame, which you can wield with ease
- A paring knife for more intricate cutting

- A mini blender. These are quite inexpensive at around the £30 mark and can quite transform your experience in the kitchen, making light of laborious tasks
- A hand stick blender. Perfect for soups, quickly whizzing marinades, and also fruit for fast bellinis
- A few baking tins. I have one of each of the following: a square tin, a round tin with a removeable base, a flan tin with removeable base, a muffin tray, a roasting tray, a baking tray
- A good quality heavy chopping board and a couple of inexpensive plastic ones for meat and fish
- Three different sized saucepans, a large and deep non-stick frying pan with a lid and a regular frying pan
- A microplane, which is perfect for zesting and grating ginger and parmesan
- A pair of kitchen tongs
- A thick pair of oven gloves
- A timer
- A mezzaluna which, frankly, makes chopping herbs and finely chopping other ingredients such as onions much more enjoyable
- I prefer non-toxic surface cleaners which are now readily available in supermarkets, or I make my own from surgical spirit and lavender
- In terms of larger equipment, I find a gas cooker much more helpful as you have much better control over temperature and can change it rapidly. If you own an electric cooker and have something on a high heat that you are bringing to the boil then need to reduce to a low simmer quickly, get another ring ready on a very low heat to transfer it straight away
- A microwave, which is great for steaming vegetables, as they retain all the nutrients inside

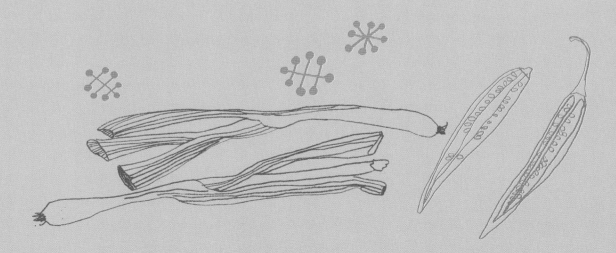

MENU PLANNER

Here are some ideas on how you might like to combine the dishes depending upon the occasion, circumstances or mood …

A LIGHT SUMMER SUPPER

Cucumber Water topped with Prosecco [199]
Plum and Coriander Ribs [96]
Clove Salt Beef with Figs, Watermelon Pepper Jelly and Radicchio [54]
Mango Ice Sticks with Dipping Sugar [142]

LATE SUMMER BARBEQUE

Paneer Rosemary Spears with Bitter Orange and Almond [63]
Red Snapper Brushed with Chipotle, Strawberry and Rosé [126]
Chargrilled Pineapple with Salted Caramel [180]

ECLECTIC INDOOR PICNIC SPREAD

Sweet Potato Mini Pasties [38]
Peach, Saffron and Tarragon Salsa served with toasted pitta bread [26]
Goat's Cheese and Pickled Chilli Dip [30]
Chorizo Crisps [26]
Chickpea Fritters with Beetroot, Buffalo Mozzarella and Pink Pepper [56]
Buttermilk-soaked Chicken with Ciabatta, Butter Beans and Brazils [51]
Elderflower Jellies with Papaya [154]
Raspberry Limeade [203]

A SMATTERING OF FRIENDS ROUND A TABLE

Watermelon Sushi with Balsamic Dipping Water [32]
Chilli Caramel Salmon Pie [91]
Sesame and Coconut Cookies with Lemon Thyme Dipping Sauce [178]

CANAPÉS FOR A COCKTAIL PARTY

Chicken Cakes with Seaweed and Lime [60]
Scallops with Bitter Lemon and Lychee [31]
Rioja Chicken with Polenta Cakes [100]
Paprika and Parmesan Chicken Skewers [132]
White Chocolate, Coconut and Redcurrant Messy Sundaes [148]
Lime, Coconut and Mint Mousse Shots [158]

ELEGANTLY EXOTIC

China tea-cups of Tiger Prawn and Mandarin Soup [44]

Sea Bass with Apple and Mint, Potatoes and Lemongrass Crème Fraiche [78]

Mandarin, Basil and Lime Sorbet [140]

SWEETLY SPICED

Goat's Cheese and Pickled Chilli Dip served with toasted pitta bread [30]

Confit of Duck Leg with Pine Nut Couscous and Date Chutney [111]

Apricot Cinnamon Fudge with Chocolate Chips served with vanilla Ice cream [163]

A HINT OF HEAT

Asparagus with Mustard Seed Cream [129]

Piri Piri- and Cocoa-rubbed Steak served with homemade chips [70]

Cardamom Chocolate Pots [161]

WARMING HARVEST BOUNTY

Roast Acorn Squash with Pear and Kiwi Chutney [58]

Baked Monkfish with Harissa and Parma Ham [113]

Roasted Vegetables with Agave, Pineapple and Mint [124]

Sweet Potato Cinnamon Fritti with Sour Cherry Syrup and Clove Maple Ice Cream [172]

RICHLY AUTUMNAL

Grilled Goat's Cheese Salad with Hazelnuts, Pomegranate and a Blueberry Dressing [30]

Leg of Lamb with Black Cherries, Tamarind and Walnut [102]

Pecan and Date Caramel Tartlets [166]

COLD WEATHER COMFORT FOOD

Ginger Chicken Soup with Lemon and Artichoke [40]

Keema, Chilli and Coriander Pie [84]

Green Raisin, Sherbet Lemon and Ginger Cheesecake [150]

GLOSSARY OF INGREDIENTS

Sometimes all it takes is the addition of one, little extra flavour which can make the ordinary taste extraordinary, and it doesn't have to be particularly expensive. Just always buy the best you can personally afford.

I have tried to include a lot of ingredients that I love throughout the book. Due to this breadth some of them only appear in one or two recipes but give them a try and start using them in different recipes and combinations:

Aduki beans
Very small, highly nutritious reddish beans with a nutty flavour, which are also used in desserts in China and Japan

Agave syrup
A low GI sweetener from Mexico that is similar to honey

Allspice
The ground powder spice of a dried berry from the Caribbean, so named because its taste has elements of nutmeg, pepper, clove and cinnamon

Anchovy sauce
A salty, umami condiment which adds a meaty depth to many savoury dishes, especially meat-free ones

Balsamic glaze
More of a balsamic syrup, this rich, thick, sticky-sweet version of concentrated balsamic vinegar goes a long way

Bitter lemon
Fizzy drink flavoured with quinine and lemon, commonly used as a mixer for spirits

Black mustard seeds
Quickly fried in oil till they pop, these impart a pungent and nutty flavour

Brown cardamom
Also known as black cardamom and large cardamom. These have a woodier, smokier flavour and taste to the gingery perfume of green cardamom, and are often used in Middle Eastern and Indian savoury rice and meat dishes

Buttermilk
Fermented cow's milk to give a refreshingly sour taste, which traditionally used to be the by-product from churning butter

Cajun spice
A delicious spice blend often including cayenne, black pepper, cardamom, cumin, oregano, chilli, coriander seed, thyme and fennel seed

Capers
Pickled flower buds sold salted or in brine

Cayenne
A hot red pepper powder that packs a punch

Chipotle paste
A barbeque-scented paste made from smoky, dried jalapenos, tomato and onion

Chorizo
A Spanish cured, often smoked sausage, flavoured with paprika. Find slices in the cold meats section of a supermarket

Ciabatta
The Italian word for slipper, this elongated light and porous bread has a deliciously crispy crust

Coconut milk/cream
Sweet, milky liquid made from the flesh of a coconut. The cream version is thicker and richer, and both are easily available in cans

Coriander seeds
The dried fruits of the coriander plant, these seeds have a warm, nutty, orangey flavour

Cumin seeds
Woody seeds which yield a warm and aromatic flavour and aroma when heated

Dijon mustard
Quite pale in colour but with a fairly strong, hot flavour

Dill
With their wispy, feathery fronds resembling fern, this herb has a mossy, aniseed flavour

Edamame
Baby soybeans sold cooked in their pods and enjoyed as a snack in Japan

Fennel seeds
Sweetly and gently anise-flavoured, these also aid digestion as well as adding crunch and contrast, especially to meats

Fish sauce
A highly pungent and salty liquid made from fermented fish but gives a deep umami flavour to Thai dishes

Garam masala
A key spice blend of Indian cooking including peppercorns, cardamom, coriander seed, cumin and cassia bark

Green cardamom
With a gingery flavour, this is a small pod with a thin green skin and pungent black seeds

Green peppercorns
These are unripe peppercorns and have a fruity pepperiness. I buy mine pickled in brine

Green pickled chillies
Whole long chillies pickled in vinegar, popular in Turkish cuisine and sold in bottles and jars

Ground bay leaf
An intense, spicy but also herby flavour. Use sparingly

Ground cloves
Whole cloves ground to make this intense flavouring

Ground ginger
With a warm, comforting spicy heat quite different to fresh ginger, this is a strong spice used frequently in baking

Groundnut oil
Made from peanuts, this mild oil can be heated to high temperatures, making it ideal for stir fries

Harissa
A stunning deep red North African paste made from chillies, garlic, cumin, coriander, tomato, olive oil, caraway and sometimes other ingredients such as rose petals

Jalapeno
Moderately hot chilli sold sliced and pickled in jars for a fruity heat

Juniper berries
Dark spicy berries that provide the well-known flavour of Gin

Kale
A hardy type of cabbage with deep forest-green curly leaves and a rich flavour

Lapsang souching tea
A Chinese tea with a distinctive smoky bacon scent

Lemon thyme
A very pretty herb with a delightful citrus flavour and scent

Lemongrass
highly fragrant, pale green grassy stalk with a lemon flavour and notes of ginger, widely used in Thai cookery

Lime leaves
Sold fresh or dried, these add an exotic citrus flavour to dishes and are a staple in Thai cooking

Lychees
Oyster-like, slippery, white-fleshed, fragrant, sweet, juicy fruit

Macadamia nuts
Deliciously creamy nuts grown in Australia and Hawaii

Maple syrup
Toffee-like sweetener made from the sap of the Canadian Maple tree

Mascarpone
Not actually a cheese but a very rich, thick cream, used in Italian desserts such as Tiramisu and also savoury dishes and as a base for sauces

Mirin
Highly sweetened Japanese rice wine, often used in teriyaki sauce

Miso paste
Japanese paste made from fermented soya beans

Muscovado
Unrefined sugar available in light brown with a fudge-like flavour and dark brown for a treacly intense sweetness.

Orange blossom water
Distilled water delicately perfumed with the essential oils of orange blossoms, used mostly in Middle Eastern cooking

Oregano leaves
Velvety soft little leaves but with a bold, peppery distinctive aroma and flavour

Palm sugar
This caramel-flavoured sugar, frequently used in Thai cooking, is made from the sap of palm trees. I use the version which is sold in tubs as granules of crystalline sugar. You find this in the World Food sections of supermarkets

Panch pooran
An Indian spice seed mix literally meaning five spices – cumin, black mustard, fennel, nigella and fenugreek

Paneer
A silky, very mild Indian cheese with a similar texture to Halloumi

Pecorino
A salty, fresh-tasting, Italian hard cheese

Pepperdew peppers
Sweet South African small red peppers, although hotter versions are also available, sold in jars in most supermarkets

Pickled ginger
Commonly used alongside sushi, this Japanese pickle gives wafer-thin slices of tangyness

Pink peppercorns
These are not the same as other peppercorns as they are actually from a different plant. Nevertheless, they are stunning and have a warm, peppery flavour

Piri piri
With African Devil being another name it is known by, this is a fiery red chilli, often crushed and sold in oil. It's popular with the Portuguese who came across it in Brazil and then took it to their African colonies

Polenta
Ready-to-eat polenta is Italian cornmeal sold in blocks in most supermarkets. I find these blocks a little plasticky so prefer to chop up, roughen the texture and remould in the preparation before cooking

Pomegranate
Sweet, sour and astringent all at once, an alluring Middle Eastern fruit used in both sweet and savoury dishes

Poppy seeds
These are nutty, tiny black grains used in both sweet and savoury dishes for bite

Poussins
Small immature chickens

Preserved lemons
Sour but fruity plump whole lemons pickled in salt and spices till soft and used widely in Morroccan cuisine

Quails
Very small game birds